ADVANCE PRAISE FOR

# *Black Theology and Youths at Risk*

"This original book is full of new ideas and practical models of ministry for all to participate in. It proposes specific steps as well as emphasizes the importance of self-love and self-reliance."

*Wyatt Tee Walker, Pastor,*
*Canaan Baptist Church of Christ*

"This book is required reading for all who have a hand in shaping the values and virtues that mold the lives of our youth. *Black Theology and Youths at Risk* is a virtual gold mine of theoretical principles and practical solutions for guiding youth today. It is the best book available that relates theology to our youth at risk."

*Noel Leo Erskine,*
*Emory University*

"David D. Mitchell has written a persuasive book that credits James Cone's *Black Theology and Black Power* as a liberating *message* for African-American youth, but nevertheless fails to chart an adequate *plan* for true liberation, such as occurred in South Africa. He then adroitly outlines a plan for readying African-American youth for authentic liberation that includes social and cultural, as well as spiritual deliverance. His focus is on Black youth because they are most vulnerable and in mortal danger of succumbing to the deadly system of DCPC ('Destructive Capitalistic Personality Complex'), which he explains. Finally, he challenges the Black church to lead the struggle."

*Cornish Rogers,*
*Claremont School of Theology*

# Black Theology and Youths at Risk

# Research in Religion and Family
## Black Perspectives

Noel Leo Erskine
*General Editor*

Vol. 5

PETER LANG
New York • Washington, D.C./Baltimore • Bern
Frankfurt am Main • Berlin • Brussels • Vienna • Oxford

David D. Mitchell

# Black Theology and Youths at Risk

PETER LANG
New York • Washington, D.C./Baltimore • Bern
Frankfurt am Main • Berlin • Brussels • Vienna • Oxford

**Library of Congress Cataloging-in-Publication Data**

Mitchell, David D.
Black theology and youths at risk / David D. Mitchell.
p. cm. — (Research in religion and family; vol. 5)
Includes bibliographical references.
1. Black theology. 2. Church work with
Afro-American youth. I. Title. II. Series.
BT82. 7.M57 230' .089' '96073—dc21 98-11294
ISBN 0-8204-4079-5
ISSN 1055-1158

**Die Deutsche Bibliothek-CIP-Einheitsaufnahme**

Mitchell, David D.:
Black theology and youths at risk / David D. Mitchell.
–New York; Washington, D.C./Baltimore; Bern;
Frankfurt am Main; Berlin; Brussels; Vienna; Oxford: Lang.
(Research in religion and family; Vol. 5)
ISBN 0-8204-4079-5

All views expressed are solely the individual author's and
do not reflect the position of any governmental agency or department.

Dedicated to my wife, Victoria Salonga. She is a source of light and strength.

Dedicated to my children, Tiffany, Ishmael, Jahrod, and Ahmad. My prayer is that they will continue to grow into loving persons committed to the service of Christ.

# Table of Contents

# Foreword

Dr. David Mitchell has placed us in his debt by chronicling for us this important book, *Black Theology and Youths at Risk.* The book is at once an exposition of Black theology as it is articulated by James Cone and an internal critique of this theology. Mitchell writes as an insider.

He is a careful student of James Cone's theology and a son of the Black church. As second generation Black theologian he raises hard questions for the practice of Black theology. He compares and contrasts Black theology as articulated by Cone with Black theology which emerged out of the South African context. Mitchell wonders why Black theology in South African benefited from a political movement supported by the African National Congress and there seems to be a political void in the case of Black theology in the United States context. Mitchell observes that the political void which Black theology in the U.S. confronts is due in part to its failure to find a following among the lower echelon in the Black community. Black theology has not been able to break out of its middle class confines. This Mitchell contends is the reason for Black theology's silence regarding the most endangered group among the oppressed; "Youths at Risk."

Mitchell forces us to examine the fact that although Black theology in the U.S. was not instrumental in founding and establishing a movement such as the Civil Rights Movement established by Martin Luther King, Jr. and Malcolm X it none the less emerged from the civil Rights Movement. The question of roots is important for Mitchell and so he presses us to ask whether or not Black theology in the U.S. has been faithful to its theological and philosophical roots. If equal rights and social justice were goals of the Civil Rights Movement of the 1950's and 1960's led by King and Malcolm X from which Black theology emerged, how are these virtues expressed in relation to youths at risk? Mitchell seems to suggest that memory must be the basis of hope. The new future must be informed by the traditions of the past. But more than this, Black theology, if it is to be service oriented towards the masses and if it is to practice kononia it must be ecclesially based. Black theology must affirm the black church as the home of theology. It is precisely at this point that Mitchell becomes praxeologically focused as he suggests that the model of ministry advocated by the Canaan Baptist Church in Harlem, New York ought to be a point of departure for

Black theological discourse that takes youths at risk seriously. Mitchell cites the mission statement of the Canaan Baptist Church which is instructive for Black theology:

> The black family is under siege internally and externally; the unhampered flow of drugs into Black communities feeds on the despair induced largely by economic injustice and internally by the deterioration of the unit and self-inflicted violence that kills Black males and children. All of this social havoc at this moment in history sits squarely on the front step of the African American Church (pp.50-51).

What is at stake is the liberation of the African-American community and Black theology as it becomes accountable to the Black community indicates the way forward. The way forward is rooted in spiritual values which press for the discernment of the demonic as well as the divine in our communities. Mitchell draws from the wells of Sojourner Truth, Malcolm X and Marcus Garvey as self-reliance becomes an important goal of Black theology. Mitchell contends that one of the errors of Black theology was to articulate its goal in negative terms—the abolition of racism—rather than values of self-determination and self-reliance. Black theology must become a tool in the hand of youths at risk for building community, moral growth and discernment. Black theology must empower our young people to take responsibility for their communities and to interpret self in the context of community.

This book is required reading for all who have a hand in shaping the values and virtues that mold the lives of our youths. *Black Theology and Youths at Risk* is a virtual gold mine of theoretical principles and practical solutions for guiding youths today. It is the best book available that relates theology to our youths at risk.

Noel Leo Erskine
Emory University

# Preface

On a personal note, growing up in the 1960s and 1970s in the midst of racial divide, social unrest, and one of the greatest cultural transitions in U.S. history, it was my spiritual awareness that established my moral foundation and the value system with which I govern my life. It was a value system that held the belief that the social circumstances in which I lived were not the will of God. This spiritual awareness was grounded in the spiritual experiences of a people struggling for liberation. Spiritual awareness gave me a faith in my Creator, an understanding of myself, and the confidence to live my purpose. I belonged to a God who had a special interest in my total spiritual and human development. Personal power is a gift to humanity from God; it is accessible to us through our faith in God, and grasp of God's love for us. In short, personal power is our spiritual ability to overcome challenges, and God as our Creator and giver of this power continues to remain intimately involved in our life experiences. God reveals God's self to us in this way everyday. Without faith personal power will become alienated from God and may become misguided and evil. My personal power was born from a faith that refused to accept the notion that my social circumstances could not be transformed. It is within this spiritual frame of reference that I write about the challenges of African-American youths at risk, and it is by returning to this spiritual frame of reference that they will find hope. I am proud to come from a faith-based Afrocentric community that reinforced in me a spiritual principle that has indelibly affected my entire life: that God did not ordain oppression in U.S. society. This principle gives hope, and is informed by one's spiritual awareness and worldview. I agree with Peter Berger who maintains that culture shapes individuals and individuals create culture. We become who we are through our culture and experiences. Family, church, schools, community, and others are significant aspects of culture; culture informs personality formation, which informs attitude, and attitude determines behavior. Spiritual awareness and worldview are crucial factors within culture that determine personality formation. Indeed, this is the developmental process that will inevitably develop the attitude which will determine individual behavior. Spiritual awareness cultivated within me a faith that recognized injustice as evil and not in keeping with the will of a loving God. My clear understanding of African-American oppression was born through my faith; this gave me new hope to visualize a better personal and community reality, and to look critically at African-American leadership and its contributions to its community's plight within U.S. society. Spiritual awareness led to my positive attitude, self-empowerment, and a faith that envisioned a better society for all. It gave me vision and focus and helped me to avoid self-destruction. Spiritual awareness led me to a constructive self-image that valued education, community and a deep sense of belonging, and a work ethic that called for one to give 200 percent. It alleviated fear. It led me to a spiritual understanding of the African-American story from slavery to freedom. It is for these reasons, among others which will be discussed later, that I came to the conclusion that spiritual awareness is that first step toward a self-liberation that will perpetuate community solidarity rather than a self-destructiveness that generates nihilism.

# Acknowledgments

This first book experience has taught me that no one finishes a book without contributions from other persons. I thank my teacher, dear friend, and mentor, Dr. Noel Erskine. I am grateful to him for a nearly twenty-year friendship that started during my theological training at Candler School of Theology, Emory University. After numerous discussions of my doctoral project, he convinced me to write this book. He felt that it was of great urgency for Black theology to clearly articulate and define to the African-American community and society at large the social dilemmas and spiritual dynamics at work among African-American youths at risk.

I thank my editor, Dr. Heidi Burns, for her encouragement and feedback. Indeed, she was extremely supportive throughout this endeavor.

I thank my mother and father, Rev. Jimmie L. Mitchell and the late Rev. Willie J. Mitchell, for their gifts of love. I will always be thankful to my dear uncle, Solomon Wilkerson, for his tough love, discipline, and spiritual wisdom, which helped shape my life.

I thank Dr. Wyatt Tee Walker, Senior Pastor of Canaan Baptist Church, for the opportunity to study Canaan's ministry to youths at risk and the African-American community. Canaan Baptist is a Christ centered church with a clear vision that understands the spiritual needs of the African-American community. The church is unique in that it has a ministry with a plan of action in place that continues to adapt to meet the needs of the community as social conditions and spiritual needs change.

I thank Dr. I. L. Mullins, Pastor of First Missionary Baptist Church in Thomasville, Georgia, my home church, for the opportunities to develop my pastoral gifts and skills under his leadership.

I thank my family, teachers, and church communities in Thomasville and Atlanta, Georgia. I cannot forget my elementary and high school principal, the late W. J. Varner. He invested a great amount of time and mentorship in me during my early development. I am grateful to Mr.

Varner and shall always cherish those years I spent with him at Douglas Elementary School and Douglas High School.

Finally, I thank my wife, Victoria Salonga, for her assistance and encouragement throughout the course of writing this book. Without her advice and tireless efforts, it would have been extremely difficult to reach my deadlines and finish this book.

# 1

# Black Theology: The Message Without a Movement

## Introduction

Black theology is the message of Christ to the poor and the oppressed. It is a message of hope and liberation for every aspect of human existence. The message of Christ as revealed in the historic Jesus is not only a message of hope for the oppressed, but it is also a mandate for a revolutionary movement of liberation for the Christian Church to carry out. If the message of Black theology does not bring life to a liberation movement within the Christian Church, it is just rhetoric; it is meaningless in the lives of those to whom it speaks. A message that does not form a plan of action to alleviate the daily struggles of human existence in a meaningful way amounts to only words with no substance for enabling the oppressed.

The historic Jesus was not merely a prophet proclaiming liberation, but his divine purpose was to come into the midst of an oppressive world to demonstrate Holy example and to teach humanity through his redemptive love, sacrificial death, and victorious resurrection the meaning of struggle to obtain ultimate hope. That is to say, Christ is the substance and the foundation for the liberation to the oppressed. According to chapter 1 of the Gospel of John, the historic Jesus was the Word made flesh or the message that initiated the ultimate movement for liberation. In other words, he was the divine power responsible for creation that became a part of creation to change the spiritual, social, political, and human condition. To put it simply, the God who creates is the God who also saves. Black theologians embrace the aforementioned chapter in the Gospel of John and Luke 4:18, to name just a few passages. These passages give credibility to the development of a meaningful theology that puts Christ in the center of the African-American experience in the U.S. in a struggle to change their spiritual, social, economic, and political condition. Therefore, Black theology is the message of Christ, and the Black Church is the means for Christ to liberate African Americans. However, the message (Black theology) must develop a strategic plan in order to empower the means (the Black Church) to rise to the challenges that lie ahead. Although some Black churches have a strategic plan of ministry in place with regard to young people, there is still a need for a well-defined national movement of Christ to eliminate oppression and usher in spiritual liberation in the African-American community focused on youths. The challenge for U.S. Black theology is to reveal the message of hope and initiate a movement for liberation at the grassroots level focused on the empowerment of youths at risk. Additionally, by centering a movement on youths at risk, real change will occur for the entire African-American community. The problem with U.S. Black theology is that it provides the message to attack racism, but it has not provided a plan of action focused on the liberation of the African-American community. However, to focus on the crucial issues of the African-American community one has to start with Black youths, particularly those at risk in society. The despair that the African-American family faces today must be alleviated, and the way to bring spiritual healing to the family is to focus on the struggles of African-American youths at risk.

This book will provide a critique of U.S. Black theology by examining the following issues:

1. The vision, passion, and function of Black theology in South Africa is examined as the message of liberation and the movement that eliminated apartheid.

2. The substance of U.S. Black theology is explored by looking critically at certain key ideas in the theology of James Cone to support my thesis that Cone's theology fails to provide the community with a clearly defined plan of action to initiate a liberation movement at the grassroots level. U.S. Black theology so far has been unable to start a movement at the grassroots level as South African Black theology did in that country. However, Cone is a superb scholar whose work emerged as the national voice, and continues to help the African-American community understand the source of its oppression even though the African-American church rejected some of Cone's ideas. However, U.S. Black theology's subsequent failure was that its war against racism was not a focused and defined practical plan that inspired unity and a national movement at the grassroots level. The fight against racism must be fought in small focused well-defined battles; it is primarily a fight against economic, political, and social oppression that are the by-products of racism. Apartheid in South Africa was a by-product of racism, and it no longer exists. However, racism

remains alive in that country. Racism is a spiritual problem that requires the right spiritual medicines to bring healing to attitudes that were shaped by ignorance and the myth of human superiority rooted in educational, family, and religious values that have been passed to White Americans for generations.

3. The complexity of the key problems that perpetuate the vicious cycle of oppression in the African-American community is outlined to substantiate that these problems are all related to the national crisis of spiritual and social oppression in which African-American youths across the U.S. find themselves trapped in an ongoing struggle to carve out a niche for themselves.
4. South African Black theology identified apartheid as its public enemy number one. By contrast, in the U.S. a public enemy number one has not yet been identified by Black theology, but this book will fill the gap by clearly identifying and defining a public enemy number one. A single identified enemy will make Black theology more relevant at the grassroots level. Cone has simply named racism as a whole the enemy.[1] Racism is too broad and complex to serve as the rallying point for a feasible and attainable movement with realistic and well-defined goals.
5. This chapter will summarize its argument and make several important recommendations that are necessary for U.S. Black theology to reestablish its vision, focus, function, and objectives. In other words, Black theology by way of the church alone will never get rid of racism in U.S. society, but it can empower the people so that they can gain the unity and passion to initiate a movement to rebuild the African-American community.
6. Finally, the sociopolitical historical backgrounds of South African and U.S. Black theologies will be compared.

This chapter does take seriously the historic and present problems of oppression as a result of the evils of racism. Racism has devastated the society of the United States at every level and continues to do so. However, the focus of this book is not the evils of racism, of which there are many, but rather the focus is a new movement by way of Black theology through the Black church to empower the whole African-American community.

## The Challenge of Black Theology in South Africa

The freedom movement in South Africa succeeded in eliminating the system of apartheid and electing a Black President, Nelson Mandela. Black theology in South Africa initiated a movement at the grassroots level that intensified on a national level and finally led to the elimination of apartheid.

In order to argue the aforementioned point, it will be necessary to closely examine the early development of Black theology in South Africa to explain how it emerged with a clearly defined objective. Its sole purpose was to end apartheid and address the crucial issues of spiritual consciousness to build a new South Africa.

In addition, U.S. Black theology emerged in the 1970s as a response to the Black power movement, a challenge to Western theology, and an interpretation of the message of Christ to African-Americans from the Black experience of oppression in the U.S., rather than emerging as an activist movement around a single crucial issue that addressed Black oppression in a nationalistic manner, as did South African Black theology when it emerged to eliminate apartheid. Instead, U.S. Black theology spread itself thin by addressing a plethora of issues, thus making it less effective.

To examine the early development of Black theology in South Africa, I will rely on the apartheid era writings of several insightful scholars who wrote essays in the book, *The Challenge of Black Theology in South Africa.*[2] These essays clearly talk about the spiritual, social, and political situation of Black South Africans living in the system of apartheid. The oppression of Black South Africans has been as complex as oppression in any culture, with the issues of jobs and economic opportunity, the lack of adequate housing, inadequate public education, institutional and social racism, substance abuse, crime, teenage pregnancy, the lack of spiritual and social self-awareness, and many others related to family security and stability. These essays consistently addressed apartheid as a point of departure for confronting all the components that perpetuate oppression in South Africa. Therefore, the authors of these essays understood South African Black theology as a movement as well as a message of hope. At the outset of the formation of South African Black theology they perceived it to become an active practical movement. There was a high expectation for South African Black theology to do something concrete about the situation in which Black South Africans lived. In the essay, "What Is Black Theology?" Basil Moore asserts that Black theologians in the United States constructed a Black theology in response to the Black power movement which later became an important aspect of the emergence of a theology of liberation. Moreover, he makes the claim that the term Black theology is an African-American phrase that is borrowed by South African scholars, but the substance of South African Black theology is vastly different from that of the United States.[3]

Moore is correct in his assertion that there are distinct differences in the Black theology of South Africa and that of the United States. Only three differences will be addressed in order to focus on the most important aspect of my argument that South African Black theology emerged as a movement to eliminate apartheid, but in the United States Black theology did not emerge with one unifying objective. Its goal has been to challenge eurocentric theology and to respond to the Black power movement of the 1970s. The following three points will be the focus of discussion:

1. Black theology in South Africa was well-defined and focused; it identified a public enemy number one (apartheid) that addressed the totality of oppression.
2. Black theology in South Africa created Black unity at the grassroots level and formed itself into a nationalistic expression of liberation.
3. Black theology came about to change cultural and theological symbols to create a new sense of spiritual consciousness and to build a new South Africa.

South Africa during its apartheid years was a nation clearly divided with a Black majority wanting freedom and a White minority desperately fighting to keep the system of apartheid intact. These essays capture the spirit of the tension that existed between the government and its Black citizens. The South African government closely monitored the activities of Black Churches and leaders and utilized tactics to prevent the teaching of ideas that threatened the existence of apartheid. These efforts by the government to stop so-called radical teachings to maintain its status quo inspired Black South Africans to embrace the very teachings that the government tried to keep them from. This tension started at the early developmental stages of South African Black theology. The government's frequent actions to prevent a national movement to end apartheid from starting had the opposite effect; it inspired the masses at the grassroots level. According to the compiler, Basil Moore, after these essays' initial publication by the University Christian Movement in 1972, they were quickly banned by the South African government, which only created a more united Black majority hungry for liberation. The political authorities viewed these essays as a national security threat. One essayist, Sabelo Ntwasa, was held under house arrest and proclaimed a serious threat to national security and good order and discipline. Sabelo Ntwasa had to withdraw as the editor, and his writings were banned from publication.[4]

The South African government's response to these essays' publication gives us some insight into the power rooted in the substance of South African Black theology and into the fear of the government that a movement for liberation was imminent. The government wanted to ensure that a movement supported by the country's majority, more than 20 million Black South Africans, did not emerge. The South African government was prepared to resort to repressive means to maintain apartheid. This, of course, was ironic; this was an excellent example of how the repressive reaction of a government ultimately contributed to the momentum of the South African Black theology movement.

When Rosa Parks refused to give up her seat on a Montgomery, Alabama, bus, the local government reacted by arresting a woman with an impeccable reputation in her church and community. The local civil rights leaders and the African-American community responded with a focused, organized, united, and impassioned protest that gained national prominence, with Martin Luther King, Jr., coming forth as the spokesman of the Civil Rights Movement of the 1960s.

The reaction dynamics between the oppressor and the oppressed in cases like these actually help to intensify protest movements and unite the oppressed. In fact, the aggressive reaction of the South African government in this and numerous other situations contributed to the South African Black theology movement's subsequent gain in popularity and power. Their response was the articulation of a national agenda, success in educating the masses, generating unity and impassioned hope, and a focused vision and its formulation as a methodology that functions with determination. The war between South African Black theology and apartheid was ignited at the earliest stages of South African Black theology's development. For several decades the African National Congress (ANC) had become a political force that aided the success of the Black theology movement at the grassroots. South African Black theology matured in substance, it became the hope, and apartheid was identified by the oppressed as public enemy number one.

The South African Black theology in these essays gave direction to Black South Africans in a desperate situation. The government's strong reaction to them indicates and affirms that Black theology was a serious challenge to apartheid. Basil Moore argues that these essays were written to initiate a liberation movement to eliminate apartheid. He writes:

> They were not written as comfortable academic exercises, nor were they written to tickle the fancy of those uninvolved in the conflict in South Africa. They were written by Black South Africans living in a situation of frightening oppression. And they were written for Black South Africans exhorting them to participate in the struggle to throw off their chains.[5]

South African Black theology's sole reason for existence was to create a liberation movement.

The vision and clearly defined focus of Black theology emerged at its earliest developmental stages because apartheid encompassed many evils interwoven in one whole system of oppression. The formation of a focus was less difficult because the complex system was captured in one single word: *apartheid.* The vision was established on the premise that there was no liberation as long as apartheid existed in South Africa. Therefore, the South African Black theology movement aided the development of the protest means, the church, and political institutions.

The substance of South African Black theology had a well-defined endeavor, proclaiming to the oppressed in South Africa and in other nations around the world that apartheid was enslaving human beings spiritually, socially, politically, and economically. This task was easy because apartheid was identified as the most oppressive system in a sophisticated world. The South African government upheld apartheid as a worthy system of government, and the word apartheid generated global attention on a nation that practiced racism as legitimate policy. South African Black theology's vision of the protest means to dismantle apartheid was a vision that the whole civilized world could embrace.

If the South African government had only perpetuated racism by red lining the Black community from economic resources, promoting job discrimination through unfair hiring practices, or by failing to adequately educate its poor citizens it would have been no different from many powerful nations, such as the United States, Germany, Great Britain, France, or Nigeria. However, because these racist practices along with many others were structurally formulated in the system called apartheid, it generated much more attention and outrage throughout the world. South African Black theology and many in the world community soon embraced the same vision, to get rid of apartheid once and for all.

In the essays in *The Challenge of Black Theology in South Africa*, edited by Moore, the function of South African Black theology is referred to as a movement to change social, political, and economic conditions by establishing a new constitution with which South Africa would be governed. This new constitution would uplift the oppressed from spiritual alienation. Moore defines the function of South African Black theology as a fight against a system, and for a people struggling for human dignity. For Moore it is an aggressive search to find meaning through the creation of new symbols to affirm Black humanity. South African Black theology is a theology that speaks for the oppressed, that emerged out of a particular experience of the oppressed, for the liberation of the oppressed.[6]

It is important to understand that South African Black theology resisted the government's hostile initiatives to stop its expansion, and this dynamic in turn produced a hostile climate. The South African government monitored Black institutions on a daily basis. Therefore, it was extremely difficult for them to function effectively as the voice for the proclamation of the word of hope, to organize strategy meetings for protest events, and to finance the movement. They spent much time reacting to an aggressive government that was consistently trying to do away with their very existence. The church is the institution where the South African Black theology movement had to originate because in political institutions all forms of expression advocating liberation were against the law. If one articulated the message of liberation in any political institution that person risked suffering a long prison sentence. Nelson Mandela went to Robben Island Prison in 1964 and spent 27 years there for opposing apartheid. The church became the only forum where the message of liberation could be proclaimed. The church was the place where South African Black theology took root and spread its message of liberation.

The function of South African Black theology in the church was crucial for another key reason: the spiritual enslavement of the oppressed could be challenged in a more meaningful way in the church. One aspect of the strategy of the South African Black theology movement was to concentrate on changing the perspective of some Black ministers who were trained by white theologians. These ministers were an important element to the overall spiritual transformation of the spiritually enslaved. According to Moore, the movement had to address this problem aggressively and swiftly to overturn a long tradition of the spiritual enslavement of Black South Africans. Therefore, a plan to influence the education of these ministers was a major function and strategy of the South African Black theology movement.[7] The preaching of a pie in the sky doctrine had to be transcended by a Gospel that proclaimed Jesus the savior of the oppressed because he was himself one of the poor and the oppressed, and his message was one of liberation and hope for those who struggle for human dignity in a dehumanizing system such as apartheid. Unfortunately, these ministers were trained and influenced by white South African scholars who did not advocate Black liberation theology. Therefore, these ministers did not have the opportunity to be taught and to grasp the Gospel of Jesus from a Black liberation perspective. However, this was the only perspective that could break the chains of spiritual bondage, and the intellect had to be freed from the chains first to promote awareness to followers. The function of the South African Black theology movement had on its side a momentum, vision, and impassioned spirit that ignited the souls of its hearers, and these ministers were no exception.

The notion of liberation was etched in the souls of Black South Africans. That is, there was a strong inspiration and an urgent desire to become free. The educated, the uneducated, the poor, the middle class, and political and religious leaders all embraced the idea that liberation was urgent and that they would have to fight with their minds, strength, souls, and intelligence to bring liberation to their lives. The South African Black theology movement emerging in what one might describe as a desperate but promising climate, made all the difference in fostering unity. South African Black theology spoke to an oppressed people who were ready to hear its message. The masses were spiritually open and tired from an era of systemic racism and totalitarianism. A new message with a new vision focusing only on the dismantling of apartheid was good news. The South African Black theology movement was cultivated on this fertile ground; from the seeds of liberation the harvest of Black unity was imminent.

Steve Biko, in his essay, "Black Consciousness and the Quest for a True Humanity," argues against the notion that Black South Africans should rely on white liberals to find a solution to the social, political, economic, and spiritual oppression of apartheid.[8] White liberals proposed a totally integrated social revolution as the best means for challenging apartheid. However, Biko argues against the notion that a liberation movement to end apartheid needed to be contingent upon white liberals' involvement. He believed that a social movement is central to the thesis, anti-thesis, and synthesis of the key problem in society. According to Biko, the white liberals understood apartheid to be the thesis, nonracism as the anti-thesis, and they had no clear definition for the synthesis.[9] Therefore, for white liberals integration was the solution because it would deal with the problem of racism while simultaneously working to destroy the evil system of apartheid. For white liberals, this would be a liberation movement involving all South African citizens against apartheid and racism. The logic behind this theory was that whites would become less racist if they were involved in the struggle for Black liberation. Biko's strategy was radically different. The goal was to obtain a unified Black humanity and a liberated Black consciousness. He understood the thesis as a strong white racism and a strong Black unity as the anti-thesis. For Biko, a movement must revolve around a unified Black front against a racist white front. According to Biko, there was no other alternative in resolving the oppression of Black Africans.[10]

The South African Black theology movement advocated Black unity as a strategy. Black South Africans were so frustrated with apartheid that Biko's message of unity was easily grasped and eagerly adopted. The South African Black theology movement emerged at a time when apartheid was aggressively fighting to stay in existence, which meant increasing repression of Black South Africans. The strength of apartheid made the South African Black theology movement more understandable and credible to the oppressed; ironically its aggression aided Black unity. Biko was among many other leaders who felt that Black unity was essential for liberation; he advocated this unity as an important strategy. Their appeal to the masses urged them to fight as a strong front against apartheid or perish weak and divided. As many embraced this message and united against apartheid, the movement spread and intensified at the grass roots.

## The Youth Crisis: A New Challenge for Black Theology in the U.S.

James Cone has provided the Black church with a theology of liberation rooted in the suffering, death, and love of Christ. He has been a genius at defining the purpose of U.S. Black theology and redefining the Black church and the church as a whole with his theology of liberation. The problem is not so much the substance of Cone's message, but how to bring alive his message of hope. What is it about Cone's Black theology that a movement of liberation failed to come about? Although James Cone's work on Black theology has been most noted and respected, there are several others who have had much to say on this subject, and whose work will be evaluated alongside Cone's.

The message of Nation of Islam leader Louis Farrakhan has stirred millions of African-American youths from all religious backgrounds as evidenced by the Million Man March in Washington, D.C. in 1995 and its anniversary in New York City. These spiritual gatherings have the potential to initiate a long-awaited movement in the African-American community. However, there is another message that's better suited for this group to advocate: the message of hope from the perspective of Christ; its primary focus must be youths at risk and self-reliance. This is the point of departure of a relevant Black theology; it offers a national plan of action to bring liberation. Such a plan has the potential to bring excitement and enthusiasm to a new movement at the grassroots level with this group at the forefront of action.

Black theology, though, has been unable to generate this kind of national interest over the past twenty plus years. However, the South African Black theology movement was able to draw enthusiastic support as pointed out above. U.S. Black theology has not developed a movement. The reasons for this will be discussed: first, by examining the social and spiritual climate of the African-American community in which Black theology emerged; second, by assessing the vision and function of Black theology and whether it was focused with a clearly defined objective that was able to perpetuate action to eliminate a specific public enemy number one.

Black theology emerged as a result of the Black power movement and during a time when African-Americans were enjoying some social and political progress as a result of the Civil Rights Movement of the 1960s. It was a time of progress, but unfortunately an era of complacency began in the African-American community soon after the passage of the Civil Rights Act, the Voting Rights Act, and the integration of public schools and other public facilities. These radical (for the time) social and political changes dulled the thirst for freedom. They gave the African-American community a sense of overwhelming success and reduced the passion that had ignited the Civil Rights Movement of the 1960s. The fire in their bellies was gone, a new agenda was not established, and the sense of direction and urgency was overshadowed by past accomplishments. This led to the weakening of African-American unity, the rise of the Black middle-class (due to new legislation that ushered in new opportunities), the development of a new underclass, and the rise of new urban ghettos. The demise of the Black power movement and the division of the civil rights leaders of the 1960s developed too many agendas. Too many leaders pursuing different agendas at the beginning of the 1970s eventually caused the premature demise of the movement that history now recognizes as the successful Civil Rights Movement of the 1960s. This movement of the 1960s lost its momentum shortly after the death of Martin L. King, Jr., which is why history refers to it as the Civil Rights Movement of the 1960s. Social progress in the African-American community from the 1970s to the present is small in comparison to that of the 1960s. A single vision for social justice has not unified African Americans and stirred them with a deep conviction around a national focus since the 1960s; King obtained a national following who supported his focus. The African-American community embraced King's vision, dream, and means to fight for justice. The change in the leadership dynamics of the African-American community changed the potential for success to continue, and this was due to too many agendas at work in the African-American community. It was in this climate that Black theology emerged.

As mentioned above, after the untimely death of Martin Luther King, Jr., many of his key followers adopted different social agendas and the Civil Rights Movement ended as it was known in the 1960s. For example, the leadership of King's successor, Ralph Abernathy, as spokesman of the Civil Rights Movement and President of the Southern Christian Leadership Conference (SCLC), was short-lived because he did not receive the same support as King. Jesse L. Jackson departed from the SCLC to start his own organization, Operation Push. Andrew J. Young won a seat in the U.S. House of Representatives and took a different course. Coretta King established the Martin Luther King, Jr., Center for Nonviolent Social Change. These events changed the direction of the Civil Rights Movement of the 1960s and contributed to bringing the African-American community to its present state of spiritual, social, economic, and political despair. The youths who grew up during this era have been the most affected and devastated by these events.

The disarray, community transitions, and the redefining of new social, political, and economic goals for the liberation of African-Americans presented the emerging Black theology with a unique challenge to emerge with a vision that all would embrace in order to create a new movement. The Black theology of Cone emerged addressing racism as the cause of the complexity of issues rather than the crucial aforementioned internal issues and external circumstances that challenged the direction and solidarity of the African-American community.[11] Additionally, Cone's Black theology did not take into account the political and social dynamics that set in motion the Black flight of the middle-class and the unfortunate development of a new Black underclass. Black theology needed to emerge with a vision that addressed all the above key concerns in order to rally the African-American community together as an effective force for liberation. However, the vision of Black theology was quite effective in putting in clear theological terms the need for a movement and the meaning of such a movement from the perspective of Christ. Noel L. Erskine, in his book, *King among the Theologians*, points out that Cone's vision for a movement of liberation was one that was rooted in the concept of Black power from a christological perspective. Erskine argues that Cone understood Black power and the power of Jesus Christ as being one and the same for African-American Christians. The traditional Black church has been rooted solely in its belief in a Christ who identifies with Black oppression and is therefore a part of the struggle for liberation. Furthermore, the use of Black power to find liberation means that Black power is Christ for African-Americans.[12] Cone believed that African-Americans became disenchanted with King and began to embrace Black power as a more realistic alternative to the message King articulated urging them to love the enemy.[13] According to Cone the enemy is definitely racism, and Black power is the necessary response to racism. However, the vision that Cone's Black theology presented perpetuated division rather than unity. As previously mentioned, the African-American community at the emergence of this early writing of Cone was challenged by numerous internal and external crises that initiated a new discourse for the community. Although Cone's message set forth to initiate a new Black power movement from the perspective of Christ, it instead made a large group of African-American Christians suspicious of a theology rooted in the radical ideas of the Black power movement. In particular, those who were followers of King and had experienced some successes from embracing the love ethic of Christ rejected Cone's position. In his book, *And the Walls Came Tumbling Down*, Ralph Abernathy affirms his belief in nonviolent direct action as a means for liberation. He writes:

> But the advocates of violence, black as well as white, had not correctly read the signs of the times and they had underestimated the strength of the organization that Martin had left behind. They had also failed to take into account my own firm resolve that what Martin stood for would be carried forward, no matter what. In the early morning hours after Martin had been shot, I called a news conference in Memphis and made our plans for the future quite clear. First, I reaffirmed our continuing commitment to nonviolence and our willingness to risk our lives for that principle.[14]

King's supporters, encouraged by their successes with nonviolent direct action, continued to employ that type of action rather than adopting Black power strategies.[15] It is significant that at the same time that Cone presented his Black theology, a new Center for Social Change to teach King's nonviolent direct action was being established. King's nonviolent direct action was adopted by the African-American community and the European-American community. This dual acceptance made it extremely difficult for Cone's Black theology to gain the support and attention needed to start a movement and to unify the African-American community.

The vision of Cone's Black theology had the substance of liberation, but it emerged at a time of tremendous social changes in the African-American community, and certain religious groups' perception of its message as too radical made it difficult for it to start a movement. In contrast, South African Black theology emerged in a radically different spiritual, social, and political climate with circumstances, mentioned at the beginning of this chapter, that promoted the emergence of the South African Black theology movement to defeat apartheid. Its vision embraced not only by Black South Africans, but by members of the world community.

Cone's Black theology articulates to the Black church and to a diverse Christian community that the church is responsible for the work of Christ. He asserts:

> Because the church is the community that participates in Jesus Christ's liberating work in history, it can never endorse law and order that causes suffering. To do so is to say yes to structures of oppression. Because the church has received the gospel-hint and has accepted what that means for human existence, the church must be a revolutionary community, breaking laws that destroy persons. It believes (with Reinhold Niebuhr) that "comfortable classes may continue to dream of an automatic progress in society. They do not suffer enough from social injustice to recognize its peril in the life of society."[16]

The Gospel of Christ is the source of authority of this ethic of liberation from which Black theology derives. The church, as the agent of Christ, becomes the only institution in which a liberation movement can emerge and be cultivated into a powerful force for transformation and hope. The church is the force of Christ in the world and its essential purpose is to function as an advocate for the oppressed.

Noel Erskine writes about Cone's ecclesiology of Black power to elaborate on Cone's understanding of how the Black church in particular, and the Christian church as a whole, should function in an effort to fight for the liberation of the oppressed. According to Erskine,

> Cone affirms the Black church as the home of theology. Because he was immensely influenced by Karl Barth, there was no doubt in his mind that theology is accountable to the church and must serve the needs of the church. But what especially fascinated him was that he found historical precedents for the Black church to be the locus and the focus of a revolutionary theology. This was important to Cone because his passion was to relate Black power to the Black church.[17]

This interpretation indicates that Black theology at its early developmental stages set forth to function as an instrument to empower the church for the initiation of a movement to do the work of Christ.

James Cone, in his book, *A Black Theology of Liberation*, argues that theology should not become a separate entity from the community to which it belongs. It emerges from and is grounded in the truth and meaning of that community's experience. It is the task of theology to inform the community of the truth of its historical existence and what the implications of these spiritual, social, political, and economic realities mean in each generation in order to keep the struggle for liberation focused and alive. According to Cone, if a community does not engage in the above mentioned discourse, it is a community that does not care what it says or does. It is a community with no identity.[18]

Cone has been a genius at defining how Black theology should function in the Black church and ultimately in the African-American community to bring liberation. The problem is that a national movement did not come about, even though the Black church is the agent of Christ where the institutionalization of Cone's Black power christology can take place. Black theology did not bring unity among African Americans or stimulate an impassioned discourse. According to Cone, it is a necessary task of theology to inform the community to which it belongs in order to keep committed followers in an ongoing struggle against oppression.[19] Did Cone's theology do this at its emergence? It identified racism as public enemy number one, but it did not establish a clearly defined function for the church to attack racism and kill it once and for all. The battle to destroy racism is a difficult task in the U.S. because it is deeply etched into the souls of some people and is projected and perpetuated daily through the images and symbols of U.S. society and some churches. Therefore, addressing solely the large scope of racism without any specificity did not provide enough focus to unify the diverse African-American community around a Black power liberation movement wrapped in christology. There are too many areas in U.S. society adversely affected by racism, and to simply attack the broad scope of racism is to spread any movement too thin. When an attack is made by any oppressed group on such a broad issue as racism in the

U.S., the passion will diminish in such an overwhelming struggle and the interest and determination of the masses will wane because it will become evident to them that they are in a lose-lose situation. Then, the struggle for liberation becomes an individual endeavor rather than a collective struggle. The pursuit of self-interest tends to replace collective struggle. There is another danger when this scenario becomes a reality: a rise in individualism that tends to take the form of capitalistic self-interest, which gives a new challenge to Black theology and the development of a liberation movement. Racism must be fought in small segments, and each little battle won is a step towards winning the overall war. What Black theology should have done and must do now is to inform the African-American community of the segment of the community most devastated by racism. Cone is correct when he holds that the task of theology is to stir the masses by defining the enemy to them in order to generate committed activists to start a liberation movement.[20] This has not happened. What should the focus for the African-American community and Black theology be?

Although there are numerous African-American institutions, communities, families, and individuals suffering as a result of the present state of the U.S. economy, the proposed solution offered by both liberals and conservatives, and many African-Americans, has been a divisive individualism rooted in capitalism. The failure of Black theology to empower the African-American church with a focused plan of action to initiate a movement has left many African-American youths devastated and out of the loop. This group of young people born in the 1970s, 1980s, and 1990s have too few individuals, politicians, or religious leaders advocating their interest; a small number of African-American churches have strong programs for the liberation of this group. Consequently, many of these young African-Americans have found their niche in U.S. society through nontraditional means with which they often cross the boundary of immoral behavior. The spiritual and moral disposition of these youths as well as their tendency to believe that they have been abandoned by the government and the leadership of the African-American community continue to perpetuate a vicious cycle of despair. This cycle of despair includes: poverty, criminal activity, gang violence, teenage pregnancy, the deterioration of the educational system, family violence and abuse, joblessness and a widespread disinterest in obtaining a job, low self-esteem, and a disproportionate number in some aspect of the U.S. criminal justice system. The necessary task of Black theology is to voice the despair of this group and inform the African-American church and community of the implications of this oppression in order to establish focus to start a new liberation movement with committed followers. As described above, there are many complex issues related to this despair of young people. Today the focus is not on Jim Crow laws as it was in the 1950s and 1960s or on apartheid as it was in South Africa, but on youths. Youths are not the enemy; young people are the victims and consequently the necessary focus of concern and the point of departure for the initiation of a new liberation movement. This recognition brings the argument closer to the point of identifying the public enemy number one of the African-American community.

The social and spiritual environment described above has had a powerful impact on these young African-Americans' worldview, moral outlook, spiritual growth, and social activity. They live in this environment desperately wanting acceptance and personal achievement but are hindered by their circumstances. Numerous anthropologists and sociologists believe that humanity creates culture, and culture shapes human personality. Millions of youths are suffering from social despair with economic and emotional anxiety and a rage toward society. They believe that in order to obtain their share of the American dream, it is necessary to employ any means. For many youths this means participating in an illegal and underground economy. The pursuit of an education is often alienated by this social despair to the point that it does not seem to be a logical or feasible course for them to take. This in turn only aggravates the economic and spiritual anxiety, the rage against society, and the deep sense of being alone and unheard. These factors have led and lead millions of youths to develop the "Destructive Capitalistic Personality Complex" or DCPC. It is rooted in anger, individualism, and immorality. This Destructive Capitalistic Personality Complex is the African-American community's public enemy number one. Black theology can initiate a new liberation movement in the African-American community if it pursues a strategic plan of action focusing on the DCPC and the environment from which it emerged. The Million Man March initiated awareness and activism among youths, and now Black theology must get to the center of this action and articulate to the African-American community how to expand this momentum, creating unity and a powerful liberation movement to bring hope to this group.

The South African Black theology movement identified apartheid as public enemy number one and South Africans at the grass roots adopted it. In the U.S., Black theology now has the same potential if it passionately focuses on the DCPC. A liberation movement with a discourse on the Destructive Capitalistic Personality Complex as the public enemy number one is attainable and will provide hope for youths and African-American communities as a whole; it will simultaneously address issues of racism that affect many other persons who are not a part of this group and inspire African Americans to activism. A liberation movement centered around the aforementioned argument in its entirety has the potential to do in the U.S. what the Black theology movement did to apartheid in South Africa.

## The Different Socio-Political Backgrounds of South African and African-American Theologies

The historical background of the African-American struggle for socio-political liberation was distinctly different from its South African counterpart. The cultural oppressions in each society resulted from completely different sets of circumstances with uniquely different histories. This historic difference had a great deal to do with the vision, focus, function, and discourse with which each of the respective Black theologies derived to reach the same goal of total liberation. African Americans were first brought to colonial America, specifically South Carolina, in 1526 by Spanish settlers. They refused to be enslaved and escaped into the interior parts of the continent, where they soon settled with Native Americans. However, during the early 1600s the system of slavery was instituted in the English colonies. Millions of Africans were brought to the United States to be slaves. In 1863 President Lincoln signed the Emancipation Proclamation declaring the end to slavery in the United States. However, an oppressive segregationist sociopolitical system kept African-Americans from obtaining equal rights and full participation in the political process. The fact that African-Americans have historically composed only thirteen percent of the U.S. population has made the struggle for liberation extremely difficult in the U.S. The Civil Rights Movement of the 1950s and 1960s granted full civil rights to African Americans in spite of their minority status and developed significant ideologies in the areas of theology and political philosophy. In contrast, South African Blacks were the majority, which was a significant advantage in their struggle against apartheid. These facts are significant to the overall success of the liberation movements for Blacks in both countries.

South African Blacks, the majority, existed in a state of freedom within an African cultural context until their land was invaded by European settlers. These Europeans instituted the system of slavery by importing West Africans in the mid to late 1600s. This system lasted until 1834, approximately forty years after the British took control of the Cape region of South Africa. The people known today as the Cape Colors are the descendants of West African slaves who intermixed with European settlers. The Dutch (Boers) defeated the native South Africans in a territorial war and founded Natal, Transvaal, and the Orange Free State territories.[21]

The British proceeded to expand their control over some of the areas previously ruled by the Dutch. This created much tension between them. A war between the British and the Dutch broke out, won by the British in 1902. By 1910, however, a unified South Africa was formed. The Dutch, though, eventually took total control of South Africa and instituted the system of apartheid that remained until 1992.

The South African Black theology movement emerged in the late 1960s and early 1970s calling for Black unity after hundreds of years of oppression and 49 years of some form of apartheid. While African Americans had some civil rights, South African Blacks were living in the midst of totally dehumanizing sociopolitical conditions. When the South African Black theology movement emerged, the South African government was aggressively oppressing South African Blacks by enforcing the laws of apartheid, intensifying the resentment of South African Blacks. By contrast, the U.S. government at this time was making advances in civil rights for African Americans; laws such as the Voting Rights Act improved the participation of African Americans in the political process. The liberating ideas and strategic protest plans of King's nonviolent direct action movement and Malcolm's Black power movement actually complemented each other, and together became significant forces that made the above civil rights gains possible. It is important to clarify that the Civil Rights Movement of the 1950s and 1960s utilized the constitution of the United States of America, specifically the fourteenth and fifteenth amendments, as well as other provisions in the U.S. constitution that pertained to the full citizenship of African Americans. Apartheid in South Africa, though, had the opposite effect on South African Blacks; it was a political system designed to keep Blacks from being recognized as full and equal citizens. Nevertheless, even without any constitution on their side the Black majority in South Africa was able to wage a successful war against apartheid. In addition, many institutions and people joined South African Blacks in the struggle against apartheid. The civil rights gains of African Americans between 1953 to 1980 can be likened to the 1992 dismantling of apartheid in the sense that the struggle is not over in either country, and that each liberation movement gained the support of many individuals of different races, nationalities, and oppressive experiences. Furthermore, while the U.S. Black minority had the U.S. constitution on its side, the South African Black majority advocated the creation of a new constitution to both end apartheid and establish full human and civil rights for Blacks.

As previously mentioned, U.S. Black theology was born during a time of tremendous sociopolitical gains. This was a time when many African Americans were enjoying the successes of the Civil Rights Movement, which bred some degree of complacency. This complacency contributed to the failure of the development of any significant movement for liberation in the past two decades. In contrast, South African Black theology appeared on the scene when Black South Africans were hungry for liberation. The word apartheid itself described the inhuman conditions of Black South Africans so accurately that it (the word apartheid) generated Black unity, and gave the movement a clear vision, focus, and function. The fight to end apartheid was supported by individuals, institutions, and some governments of the world community.

# 2

# African-American Youths at Risk: The Destructive Capitalistic Personality Complex

The Destructive Capitalistic Personality Complex (DCPC) is the number one threat to the African-American community and to youths in particular. The sociospiritual culture into which these young persons were born in the 1970s, 1980s, and early 1990s has been the DCPC's twin in this crisis. The DCPC is not a psychological disorder inherited through one's family genes. Rather, it is obtained through an oppressive socialization process and numerous factors aid its development.

The DCPC is the number one threat to the African-American community. Youths with the DCPC live by a mean-spirited code of conduct often obtained through gang relations. In fact, when the DCPC is acquired youths assume an iniquitous character. The DCPC does not discriminate; youths across the social spectrum are at risk to acquire it. Whether youths come from a broken family orientation or a well principled, moral, and spiritual family orientation they become at risk to obtain this unethical character in the above mentioned socialization process. Youths who lacks self-confidence and self-esteem are easy prey in this unfortunate social despair. In addition, the DCPC is acquired through peer pressure. A street-smart mindset is established in these youths, and they take on a criminal lifestyle, in which they use quick money making schemes as their means to live. With its materialistic, destructive, and anti-society worldview, it indoctrinates youths with a negative character that determines the way youths think and act. Thousands of young persons adopt a negative character that employs anti-society values for economic survival and to obtain their desire for immediate self-gratification in the form of material gain. As a result, they lack the value of individual responsibility to help bring harmony, wholeness, and liberation to the African-American experience; adopting DCPC unethical practices has left them without spiritual awareness, which has been profoundly devastating to the African-American community. A cycle of oppression sets forth, causing the development of the underclass, dysfunctional families, violence, and crime. The DCPC takes root in youths as a survival mechanism, indoctrinating them to negative values and a street wise alternative to gaining wealth as they search for meaning in a capitalistic society rooted in racism, individualism, social and spiritual despair, and family dysfunction. In his book, *Race Matters*, Cornell West describes the nihilism which is widespread among the African-American community. He asserts,

> Nihilism is to be understood here not as a philosophic doctrine that there are no rational grounds for legitimate standards or authority; it is, far more, the lived experience of coping with a life of horrifying meaninglessness, hopelessness, and (most important) lovelessness. The frightening result is a numbing detachment from others and a self-destructive disposition toward the world. Life without meaning, hope, and love breeds a cold-hearted, mean-spirited outlook that destroys both the individual and others.[22]

I would have to agree with West's understanding of nihilism. However, some individuals respond differently to this sociospiritual despair, and despite all adversity live a spiritually and morally meaningful life under the worst of social circumstances. They live in unfortunate social circumstances with a strong sense of spiritual meaning as was evidenced in slavery, and is being evidenced today among many elderly, middle-aged, and young persons. Many African-American youths, predominantly male, respond to this despair with aggression, protest, and the determination to survive and succeed at any cost. The end result is an inhuman temperament and a self-destructive way of living in order to achieve a sense of success within a worldview that has little regard for others and no moral boundaries; this is what I have defined as the Destructive Capitalistic Personality Complex or the DCPC. The demand, "I just want to get paid," becomes the negative code by which these individuals conduct their lives. The DCPC is easily adopted by persons who see themselves as victims, and are left behind and out of the loop in a society that treats them with inhuman indifference. They believe that society left them to fend for themselves with no resources. The DCPC allows them to achieve a sense of immediate economic and social gratification in the here and now. The DCPC gives them an overwhelming sense of power and pride, respect among peers, and inspires them to become skilled in this dangerous way of life, and they become at risk for catastrophic personal disasters. For many youths this status and sense of somebodiness is a social promotion in comparison to what they had before, which was only social oppression. Youths who adopt the DCPC lifestyle participate in criminal activities that put them at risk of imprisonment establishing a criminal record, premature death, physical harm, drug addiction, and destroyed families. These persons are looking for a shortcut to material success. The DCPC tends to make its victims believe that the life that they have adopted is the only viable alternative for survival. However, the sense of success that comes from this immorality and destruction is short-lived. These youths are filling American prisons to capacity and are losing their lives at alarming rates.

Spiritual awareness, love from family and community, and education at church and school are the things that will ultimately give meaning and hope to this at risk generation. These institutions help to establish and form a person's spiritual values, moral outlook, and sense of esteem and belonging. These concepts in turn lay the foundation that will determine an individual's course in life. The lack of spiritual meaning, education, and a sense of belonging and connection to a larger community leaves one feeling alone and more vulnerable to the influences of the sociospiritual despair that at present is widespread in the African-American community. The DCPC is easily acquired when at this vulnerable state of mind and spirit; it is the number one threat to the overall healing and economic development of the African-American community because it brings hundreds of thousands of young at risk and vulnerable persons to an immoral existence and an aggressive search for economic hope. These youths embrace a life of crime, violence, prostitution, and they lose any previous sense of spirituality that they may have had. This acquired DCPC attitude is one that lives by these words that have become a chorus in communities across this nation, "I just want to get paid." There is no other threat in the African-American community that has devastated the family, the church, and schools since the 1970s as the DCPC has; it has been destructive in all areas of black existence. Historically, racism was destructive, but it did not destroy the strong spiritual awareness and moral responsibility that survived the worst racist social and economic circumstances. The DCPC takes away young people's hope for the future by destroying core spiritual values, by youths' acceptance of DCPC negative practices, and by the DCPC youths who promote violence and perpetuate peer pressure in the African-American community. The DCPC is adversely affecting the key institutions that promote spiritual meaning and stability in the African-American community.

## Nihilism and the DCPC: A National Epidemic

The ubiquitous violence and crime among young African Americans across the U.S. significantly demonstrate the magnitude of widespread self-destruction. How did this social despair become a national crisis and what is the solution to it? Widespread violence among African-American youths is a result of the DCPC undergirded by a powerful drug culture and gang activity at work when these at risk young people try to find hope and a niche in society by any means available. A social despair conducive to the development of a self-centered mindset perpetuates violence and crime. A mean-spirited and cold-hearted attitude are the prerequisites for the DCPC. When a young person acquires the DCPC, an immoral worldview replaces spirituality and previous moral values. There are no ethical boundaries in the quest for material gain. Working to eliminate the DCPC with both spiritual values and practical action is the solution to the problem. Alleviating the DCPC is the challenge for the Black church because it has the moral and spiritual authority to meet this challenge with formidable odds. The church was the rallying place and the vehicle that helped to bring social change during the civil rights eras of the 1950s and 1960s.

Deborah Prothrow-Stith points out that youth violence in the African-American community has become a national epidemic and is the number one cause of death of poor African-American males. She claims that social despair and the ghetto culture in which these youths live have a profound influence on their psyche and is the root cause of their angry and rampant self-destruction.[23] Prothrow-Stith maintains that this anger results from a sense of hopelessness and meaninglessness. That is, being poor in a nation where acquiring wealth is regarded with utmost importance alienates many and reinforces the development of their anger. Being a victim of racism, attending a school where one's intelligence level is often prejudged as being below the norm, and facing a future without professional fulfillment are factors which can lead African-American youths to anger.[24] She asserts:

> I intuitively believed that the social context was as important as the family setting. Moreover, I sensed that the social setting could play a role in a young person's failing to develop adequate ways to handle his own aggression. Living in a violent environment in which aggressive outbursts were common, I tended to think, could encourage displays of aggression that in another, more peaceful environment might well have been contained.[25]

The environment in which many young African Americans live is one of social despair where it has become too common to live by the ethic that becoming wealthy is the ultimate form of freedom and liberation. More importantly, the DCPC negative ethic focuses on obtaining wealth at any risk. Living in hopeless and meaningless social conditions in a nation where great value is placed upon wealth results in resentment in many African-American youths. They also aspire to be affirmed and valued and to experience the same sense of somebodiness and achievement as defined by American society, which places prime importance on succeeding in a competitive capitalistic culture. However, the likelihood of these youths becoming economically successful through legitimate means is limited by poor education, the lack of role models, and the lack of encouragement and information. Prothrow-Stith suggests that the social despair prevalent in the environment is the primary reason for the violence of the African-American youth. It does seem logical in true in this crisis, that as poor persons in a society where wealthy persons are valued and poor persons are not, some of the poor will become angry and aggressive. What do these young angry men need in order to become liberated? These angry young men, just like anyone else, need a sense of spiritual identity and a sense of community belonging and social achievement. Furthermore, there is an anti-establishment sentiment deeply rooted within this angry at risk group, and many of these youths believe that much of their violence is necessary for survival because much of mainstream business is not open to them. With this perception at the core of their worldview, their search for achievement and survival often lead them outside the mainstream economy. These young African-Americans believe that they live in a racist society in which the rules of the game are written in a language that they cannot understand or speak, in which they are discriminated against and are not afforded an equal opportunity. In addition, youths at risk believe that in American society they cannot acquire the wealth necessary for a sense of worth through moral means. Consequently, for many the alternative road to wealth is the DCPC way of life.

Violence is responsible for 20,000 homicide deaths in the United States each year and for leaving many others severely injured. Many of these victims are young and poor African-Americans.[26] The former Surgeon General of the U.S. from 1981-1989, Dr. C. Everett Koop, in the introduction to *Deadly Consequences*, maintains that in 1984 he startled many Americans when he adopted the public health policy that violence is as much a public health issue as many dangerous diseases.[27]

I concur with Prothrow-Stith and Weissman's notion that violent behavior is often the result of social despair and an environment in which violence is a daily occurrence. Furthermore, the lack of spirituality and the importance placed upon wealth is the deadly combination responsible for much of this nihilism and violence. The widespread social despair, the racism that causes joblessness and leaves many with a deep sense of rejection and victimization by society, the importance placed upon wealth, the sense of being alone in a competitive capitalistic system, and, most importantly, the lack of spirituality necessary to maintain a sense of wholeness and somebodiness in the midst of overwhelming despair leave these young persons vulnerable. This is when the DCPC appears to be the only alternative. People who have the Destructive Capitalistic Personality Complex (DCPC) employ violence to obtain material gain and a sense of worth.

## The Drug Business and the DCPC in Action

The rise of drug abuse and trafficking in the African American community are responsible for the development of widespread social despair and nihilism and have triggered an ongoing cycle of crime, violence, gang activity, teenage pregnancy, and broken families. These complex social problems are all the cause of the DCPC. The drug trade is a huge business in the U.S., generating billions of dollars each year. Large amounts of crack cocaine are concentrated in African-American neighborhoods across the country, and many youths enter this business in an effort to fulfill their dreams of gaining a sense of value by earning a big amount of fast money. Many of these young people live in poor neighborhoods where the drug business is prevalent, violence is a daily occurrence, and the fast rewards and glamour of the drug trade are more attractive than legitimate ways to find meaning, hope, love, a sense of value, and a livelihood. For these young men money means a sense of worth and respect in their neighborhoods. However, many die young or become incarcerated. Prothrow-Stith and Weissman provide evidence that death, imprisonment, and serious physical injury are the end results of involvement in the drug business.

Prothrow-Stith and Weissman write about the tragic life of a young New York City drug dealer, Preston Simmons, who was shot with a 9-millimeter automatic pistol nine times by four young men who were rival drug dealers as he walked from his girlfriend's house to his house.[28] The DCPC is evidenced in such violent outbursts where money and drugs are the motive. Prothrow-Stith and Weissman assert:

> The booming traffic in illicit drugs, most especially cocaine and its derivatives, has introduced near anarchy into hundreds of poor urban areas all over the country. In these beleaguered neighborhoods drug dealers have cowed and silenced the majority of poor and working people. . . . The simplest assumptions of civilized life that parent and child will be able to walk down the street unmolested, that a child will return home safely from school are denied them. Their reality is automatic weapons fire, shootouts, crossfires, and the fear of stray bullets.[29]

Prothrow-Stith and Weissman are on the right track when they assert how the drug business has endangered African-American social existence, but one needs to go a step further. In fact it is a specific entity, the DCPC, that is largely responsible for the development of the drug business in the African-American community. The DCPC takes root within those youths whose attitudes and behaviors are formed in nihilistic social environments where many have reverence for the drug business because it offers economic security. In their search for economic well being and esteem DCPC youths develop immoral principles to govern them. Many young persons pursue this self-destructive path because they have concluded that it is the only means to wealth that appears feasible. Additionally, Prothrow-Stith and Weissman make the argument, and I agree, that the drug problem must be understood from a broad perspective because it adversely affects all areas of social existence. It is a job problem, a housing problem, a family problem, and a spiritual and moral problem.

The crack cocaine epidemic that exploded in African-American communities in the 1980s brought with it a profound nihilism: Gang-related violence spread rapidly as many gangs were able to organize themselves, earn large sums of money, gain access to weapons, and control entire neighborhoods as their territory. Neighborhoods became war zones when there were territorial disputes between opposing gangs, and African-Americans were nearly always the victims and the perpetrators. There is now an African-American generation ignorant of the spiritual values that sustained the community from slavery to the civil rights struggle of the 1960s. Prior to the 1980s cocaine was the drug of the rich, but recent studies have revealed these facts: (1) crack was developed as a more addictive and cheaper form of cocaine and was introduced to the U.S. in the 1980s in South Central Los Angeles; (2) crack was developed and introduced to the U.S. as an affordable drug for the poor; (3) initially it appeared only in African-American neighborhoods; and (4) the crack business has aided the organizational development and financing of gang activity in the African-American community across the U.S.

During the late 1960s and early 1970s the Black Power Movement led numerous education initiatives in Oakland, Chicago, and other major cities across the U.S. to prevent drug use. They sponsored community campaigns to educate African-Americans that it was their responsibility to keep drugs out of their communities and drug use from becoming an epidemic. However, their effort to stop drugs from coming into the African-American community ended with their demise. The demise of the Black Power Movement in the late 1970s has left poor African-American neighborhoods vulnerable to increased drug abuse and trafficking. African-Americans are still responsible for the existence of this social and spiritual epidemic. DCPC acquired youths are responsible for creating and maintaining a drug culture that is more destructive than slavery or the Jim Crow laws of the post-Civil War era. Neither slavery nor the social degradation of the post-Civil War era was able to destroy the spirituality of African-Americans. These were the worst social conditions that any people in the history of the U.S. have ever suffered. However, African-Americans were able to keep their spiritual focus; it was rooted in a dignity poised with a strong faith and perseverance that only death could silence, but it would rise again in those they inspired.

Since the 1980s the deadly crack-cocaine has been on the streets of the African-American community, and gangs across the country and their associates have made millions. These criminal organizations prey on and are still destroying African-American youths at risk. As stated earlier, the DCPC is the number one threat to the African-American community because it has replaced spiritual values with destructive and unethical values. In fact, in the 1980s nihilism exploded in the African-American community when, ironically, the crack business and its violence invaded the African-American community through urban gangs.

The large cash flow and the sense of identity gangs provided made them attractive to young men. According to Prothrow-Stith and Weissman, the drug business has become a major employer of the young in cities across the nation.[30] They work as lookouts, warning dealers that the police have been spotted. They work as stash guards, guarding stored drugs. They work as layaways, holding drugs. They work as touts, promoting a dealer's brand of drugs. They work as delivery boys, transporting drugs. These young people have the potential to earn hundreds of dollars a day, a fact that attracts many. The consequences to the African-American community are indicated by the following statistics from the 1996 edition of *Black Americans: A Statistical Sourcebook*. There were 3.7 million African-Americans arrested in 1994 and 288,133 of these arrests were for violent crimes; 10,420 were murders, and 62,628 were committed by African-Americans under the age of 18, according to the U.S. Federal Bureau of Investigation. According to the U.S. Justice, Bureau of Justice Statistics, as of December 31, 1993, 456,570 African-Americans were incarcerated in prisons; 426,401 being housed in state institutions, and 30,169 in federal institutions. African-Americans make up less than 13 percent of the U.S. population, but about 48 percent of the prison population.[31]

Black theology must address these issues in an effort to empower the African-American church with a strategy and plan of action to increase spiritual awareness. This spiritual awareness would lead the entire African-American family in a spiritual liberation movement to destroy the DCPC by transforming the youth with spiritual and moral values. Black theology and the Black church have the most important role in the effort to destroy the African-American community's public enemy number one, the DCPC, with a practical plan of action. The future of many youths hinges on how the African-American church and community respond to this threat. In the past several decades, Black theology has informed African Americans of the adverse implications that racism has upon the spiritual and social quality of life of the American-American community. The problem with Black theology since it came on the scene in the early 1970s is, it has focused on the destruction of racism in an effort to bring social transformation, and this will be mentioned in detail later. This preoccupation with racism was at the expense of spiritual and moral development. Black theology must now speak to the despair that youths face, and specifically those youths at risk to acquire the DCPC if it is to become the relevant theology of the total African-American community.

# 3

# U.S. Black Theology: A Historical Perspective

## The Historical Roots and Influences of U.S. Black Theology

U.S. Black theology emerged during the 1960s to challenge the theological and ethical positions of Western theology in response to the Civil Rights Movement and the Black Power Movement. In his book, *A Common Journey: Black Theology (USA) and Latin American Liberation Theology*, George L. Cummings asserts that Black theology is grounded in the history of the political, economic, social, and personal sufferings of African-Americans, and cannot be understood or evaluated apart from that history. The African-American community's determination and capacity to understand christology in light of its experience of suffering and oppression in the U.S. empowered its search for meaning and hope. Consequently, Black theology emerged in the 1960s as a product of African-American faith in response to a history of struggle and oppression.[32]

The 1960s in the U.S. was a time of unrest and the Civil Rights Movement emerged with a Black theology that gave voice and shape to social and political concerns. The struggles of the 1960s merely built upon a religious tradition with roots in slavery that reported God as liberator. The faith tradition that held that all human beings were created equal, and that slavery or any form of injustice was not the will of God, started in the midst of sweltering oppression on the slave plantations; it was the faith tradition upon which Black theology build upon. George Cummings asserts:

> From the very beginning of their enslavement in white Christian America, blacks began to reflect on the meaning of their faith in the light of their religious experience, and to assert that slavery was not Christian. Indeed, black religion, understood as all those religio-cultural sensibilities and values African, European, and American, functioned as the fulcrum of protest against black oppression . . . . black slaves sought to understand their faith and to find the resources for survival.[33]

The emergence of Black theology in the 1960s and its continued development into a universally acclaimed theology, expanding into new arenas with fresh ideas and addressing important issues on behalf of the oppressed with new approaches and methods for liberation, would not be possible were it not rooted in this strong faith tradition. This faith tradition has been an important factor in the development of strong families, churches, and institutions in the African-American community, and is one source of strength that social degradation has been unable to destroy. A faith tradition that was able to critique a racist christology without formal theological training was a unique accomplishment. This is not to suggest that the slaves constructed a formal Black theology. However, they initiated a faith tradition that for several centuries has empowered the African-American struggle for justice and has been a positive spiritual force in the Black experience. According to Cummings it was because the slaves interpreted their faith in light of their oppression that they were able to find resources for survival. However, one needs to go a step further and assert that the slaves were able to establish and pass on a faith tradition that would empower and sustain them and succeeding generations in numerous struggles for liberation.

In his book, *Xodus: An African-American Male Journey*, Garth Baker-Fletcher argues that certain slaves were theologically sophisticated in their biblical exegesis and in their practice of the strong faith tradition that was started by slaves. Baker-Fletcher states that a former slave, Henry Bibb, wrote to his former slave owner, Albert Sibley, using biblical authority to argue against the institution of slavery and to critique the Methodist church. Bibb wrote:

> While on the other hand your church sanctions the buying and selling of men, women, and children; the robbing of men of their wives, and parents of their offspring the violation of the whole of the decalogue, by permitting the profanation of the Sabbath; committing of theft, murder, incest, and adultery, which is constantly done by church members holding slaves and form the very essence of slavery. Now, Sir, allow me with the greatest deference to your intelligence to inform you that you are miserably deceiving yourself, if you believe that you are in the straight and narrow path to heaven, whilst you are practicing such abominable violations of the plainest precepts of religion.[34]

Bibbs' written critique of the Methodist church and his former slave master is one example among many of how the theological thinking of many slaves, which was rooted in a radical faith tradition, was sophisticated to say the least. The faith tradition that African-Americans inherited from their slave ancestors continues to shape African-American religious experience today; it is at the core of Black theological thinking and religious practice and will remain a central part of each of these because African-Americans remain a people who understand their oppression in light of their faith tradition. This slave faith tradition played a key role in inspiring revolts and movements against slavery and oppression as evidenced by the actions of men such as Gabriel Prosser, Denmark Vesey, and Nat Turner. They were key subjects in the formation of the Black theology that emerged in the 1960s.

## Black Theology in Action: Martin Luther King, Jr., and the Civil Rights Movement

The Black theology practiced by Martin Luther King, Jr., during the Civil Rights Movement of the 1950s and 1960s continues to shape and influence Black theology. King's theology has its roots in the same faith tradition that was shaped and cultivated by African-American slaves who understood God as liberator. The Civil Rights Movement which was led by Martin Luther King, Jr., was a freedom movement against African-American oppression grounded in the Christian faith. The radical faith grounded in the love ethic of Christ practiced by King and his followers challenged the white Christian church, the Constitution of the U.S., and racist practices of U.S. society. More importantly, King's Black theology made a prophetic call upon African-American churches to put into action the values of a strong faith tradition that opposes oppression. The African-American Christian community adopted King's vision and theological approach to fight injustice. In his book, *God of the Oppressed*, James Cone makes the point that King's fight against oppression was rooted in the religious tradition of his slave ancestors. Cone asserts:

> The identification of divine justice with civil justice became the central theme of the civil rights movement in the 1950s and 60s. This identification was consistent with black religious tradition and with the Bible. To justify his fight against injustice, Martin Luther King, Jr., referred not only to the Exodus and Jesus Christ, but specially to the prophets of the Old Testament.[35]

Cone established that King's fight for freedom and justice for African Americans was grounded in the strong faith tradition of suffering African Americans. King was in the same religious tradition as many African-American ministers and activists who had fought against African-American oppression as far back as slavery. In fact, King was of the same religious tradition as Henry Highland Garnet, whose prophetic voice spoke to slaves. Cone asserts that Garnet epitomized the spirit of the black religious tradition when he identified obedience to God with struggling against slavery. Garnet said:

> Your condition does not absolve you from your moral obligation. The diabolical injustice by which your liberties are cloven down, neither God, nor angels, or just men, command you to suffer for a single moment. Therefore, it is your solemn and imperative duty to use every means, both moral, intellectual, and physical, that promises success.[36]

Garnet's prophetic message to slaves is the same one that King spoke to African Americans. Garnet spoke of the same moral imperative to fight against injustice that King did in the 1960s. King's moral imperative urged European-American Christians to chose good rather than evil, love rather than hate, justice rather than injustice, and equality rather than discrimination.

In the famous "Letter from a Birmingham Jail," King informs local white clergy, who urged him to end his protest in Birmingham, that his action and call for the end of injustice and segregation in Birmingham were motivated by and rooted in a Christian faith tradition. King asserts:

> I am in Birmingham because injustice is here. Just as the prophets of the eighth century BC left their villages and carried their "thus saith the Lord" far beyond the boundaries of their home towns, and just as the Apostle Paul left his village of Tarsus and carried the gospel of Jesus Christ to the far corners of the Greco-Roman world, so am I compelled to carry the gospel of freedom beyond my own home town. Like Paul, I must constantly respond to the Macedonian call for aid. Moreover, I am cognizant of the interrelatedness of all communities and states. I cannot sit idly by in Atlanta and not be concerned about what happens in Birmingham. Injustice anywhere is a threat to justice everywhere.[37]

King's response to the white clergy in Birmingham indicated that his nonviolent protest was not only in harmony with the God of the Christian faith, but that he and his followers were actually inspired by God to resist the evils of a racist society. He pointed out that his action was grounded in the same gospel and faith tradition as that of the biblical prophets and the Apostle Paul, and was, therefore, in the same spirit. King understood Christianity from a theological perspective immersed in the notion that the Christian God of the Bible was directly opposed to injustice, racism, and the inhuman treatment of African-Americans. Additionally, King pointed out that his Christian faith was his moral authority and the basis for teaching his followers that it was Christian to oppose injustice.

Black theology must advocate the radical involvement of African-Americans in their community, and the African-American church is critical in determining the success of such involvement. If Black theology cannot attract

African-American church leaders, it cannot wage a successful movement. King correctly attracted church ministers and leaders to the movement, and with their unity they were able to wage a movement against racism. The Civil Rights Movement led by King was in fact Black theology in action, and was successful. The relevance and success of Black theology hinges on its ability to ignite a movement through the participation of the African-American church. Either Black theology has been unable to stimulate this type of involvement or the church has been unwilling to hear its entire message and call for radical involvement. As previously mentioned, the Black theology of the 1960s and early 1970s was partially rejected by the church. The church and Black theology are equally responsible for the development of a plan of action to bring liberation to the African-American community. U.S. Black theology needs to serve the church more meaningfully in the future by proposing a concrete plan of action to oppose an identified public enemy number one rather than racism at large; these are shortcomings in both U.S. Black theology and the African-American church that must change. The church model of ministry discussed in more detail later lays out a plan of action for the African-American church rooted in Black theology and the African-American faith traditions. If the church rejects a plan of action that has vision, focus, and a function, the church would be the problem, not U.S. Black theology. Racism is too large a target to attack, which has been Black theology's endeavor since its beginnings. The South African Black theology movement's and the Civil Rights Movement's action-oriented theology can inform U.S. Black theology on practical vision, focus, and function, in its continued struggle for spiritual and social transformation. Furthermore, when this takes place, U.S. Black Theology will mature from its present theoretical disposition to a practical and relevant plan, which will make it applicable to the everyday problems of oppression in the African American experience. Martin Luther King, Jr.'s Black theology was not only grounded in the same religious tradition as that of his slave ancestors, but it was Black theology in the technical and intellectual sense. King's writings, sermons, and speeches are valuable documents for theologians for years to come. When Black theology came about in the 1960s King was a key element in its development. Today scholars debate whether King was a theologian in the traditional sense. In fact, King's theological training and practical theology set new standards and broke new ground in Black theology. King was a trained theologian who applied his theology to the Civil Rights Movement. In his doctoral dissertation at Candler School of Theology, Emory University, *Martin Luther King, Jr. as a Theologian of Radical Involvement*, Luther Ivory argues that King was a theologian who advocated a faith of radical involvement against oppression and injustice. Ivory asserts:

> King is best understood as a creative theological thinker who offered a theology of radical involvement. King's theological perspective sought to raise permanent, generative tensions for the culture of his day. At the same time, it sought to resolve those tensions in light of a radical, Christian vision that was thoroughly informed by a notion of "the radicality of involved love." King's social activism was based upon an ethic of community, and this ethic was informed by structured theological formulation on how love radically involves itself in the affairs of human history.[38]

King's Black theology was a departure point for the Black theology that emerged in the 1960s. Indeed, King was a theologian who advocated a theology of radical involvement. It was grounded in his radical faith tradition that began with his slave ancestors and which had a deep understanding of the love ethic of Christ as a radical involved love that would go to great and difficult lengths to liberate humanity and establish the beloved community.

### Malcolm X and Radical Black Power Theology

Black theology originated during the tumultuous 1960s in response to the Black Power Movement that was supported by many African Americans. The ideas of Malcolm X were at the center of Black Power philosophy, which addressed the issues of Black self-love, Black unity, and racism, stimulating many theological discussions. Ironically, the influence of Malcolm X's ideas also reached people immersed in the Christian faith tradition. The Black theology of the 1960s emerged with the authentic substance of the Black Power ideology. In his book, *The Common Journey*, George Cummings asserts:

> While it is important to view Martin Luther King, Jr. and the Civil Rights Movement as an important factor in the development of BTUSA, BTUSA owes an even greater debt to Malcolm X and the Black Power Movement. BTUSA owes its origin to the struggle for black empowerment amid a world of suffering and powerlessness, and behind the Black Power Movement stood the presence of El Haj Malik El Shabazz (Malcolm X).[39]

Malcolm X's Black Power ideology had a profound impact on Black theology.

Malcolm was a minister in the Nation of Islam under the leadership of Elijah Muhammad, but he later in life departed from the teachings of

Muhammad to adopt the more traditional Islamic faith and theology. However, Malcolm X, like Martin Luther King, Jr., was also a product of the Christian faith tradition that was passed on by his slave ancestors. Malcolm and King came from a faith tradition that understood God as liberator. Malcolm X's father was a Baptist minister with a Black nationalist view that was profoundly influenced by Marcus Garvey's notion of black nationalism. Malcolm's early spiritual formation was shaped by Garvey's and his father's views. Malcolm's early religious experience in his home must be taken seriously to understand the origins of his philosophy. Malcolm X was essentially grounded in the same faith tradition as most African Americans. Malcolm was more mature as a Muslim minister than as a young Baptist, but the fact remains that he learned to understand the oppression of African Americans in light of his faith traditions, which held God as liberator. The slave faith tradition opposed oppression in light of their belief that God was a God of justice, liberation, and love. From his Muslim perspective, Malcolm X believed that Allah was a liberator who was against the dehumanization of Black personhood, a belief that was similar to the Black Christian perspective of God. The religions were different, but both were applicable in the fight against the same enemy, racism. Malcolm maintained that African Americans must be proactive in their search for liberation. Malcolm asserts:

> The American black man should be focusing his every effort toward building his own businesses, and decent homes for himself. As other ethnic groups have done, let the black people, wherever possible, however possible, patronize their own kind, hire their own kind, and start in those ways to build up the black race's ability to do for itself. That's the only way the American black man is ever going to get respect. One thing the white man never can give the black man is self-respect! . . . The black man needs to start his own program to get rid of drunkenness, drug addiction, prostitution. The black man in America has to lift up his own sense of values.[40]

Black theology, of which Malcolm X's thinking is a part, advocates self-empowerment.

Malcolm championed the spiritual value of self-love, which he viewed as essential for the liberation of African Americans regardless of religious faith. His advocacy of self-love was an urgent call for the radical involvement of all African Americans to increase Black self-respect, dignity, and to become self-reliant. In his book, *Xodus: An African American Male Journey*, Garth Baker-Fletcher expounds on Malcolm's notion of self-love. He asserts:

> Malcolm believed that self-respect had been systematically stripped away from American Blacks by the European-American system of racism, or the collective white man. Malcolm dramatized in vivid language the way in which the "white man" had brutalized, raped, and robbed the "black man" of self-respect, pride, and dignity. In fact, according to Malcolm, the "white man" literally brainwashed African people into "so called Negroes." The "Negro," according to Malcolm, had become sickened psychologically, spiritually, emotionally, economically, and politically by accepting self-hatred into our collective psyche.[41]

The central theme of Malcolm's vision, message, and mission was for the radical involvement of African-Americans in a united struggle for liberation by championing Black self-love and self-respect. Malcolm believed that African-Americans had suffered the worst and profoundest oppression, the robbing them of their sense of self-worth. Malcolm asserts:

> Your slavemaster, he brought you over here, and of your past everything was destroyed. Today, you do not know your true language. What tribe are you from? You would not recognize your tribe's name if you heard it. You don't know nothing about your true culture. You don't even know your family's real name. You are wearing a white man's name! The white slavemaster, who hates you!....You are the planet Earth's only group of people ignorant of yourself, ignorant of your own king, of your true history, ignorant of your enemy! You know nothing at all but what your white slavemaster has chosen to tell you. And he has told you only that which will benefit himself, and his own kind.[42]

Malcolm's Black Power ideology had a primary influence on the Black theology that emerged in the 1960s, and will continue to shape Black theology in the years to come. Baker-Fletcher's realizes that Malcolm's notion of human dignity and self-respect deserves equal credit as that of King's thought. Malcolm X's notion of self-love and King's notion of somebodiness are very similar.[43]

## Black Womanist Theology

Black Womanist theology is a Black liberation theology that brings into focus crucial issues related to gender oppression, family, church, and community that are essential to the ongoing struggle for liberation in the African-American community. Black theology of the 1960s failed to address the gender oppression of African-American women. Gender oppression hinders the liberation and healing of the African-American family, church, and community.

When Black theology first came about in the late 1960s and early 1970s its focus was on white racism. It set forth to inform the African-American community of the implications of racism on African-American life and to engage the community in a struggle to fight racism. It neglected African-American women's gender oppression in the church and community. The implications are devastating not only to African-American women, but to the youth, family, church, and the community as a whole.

Black theology's central argument against racism was informed by its traditional understanding of the doctrine of humanity, that God created African Americans as human beings with the same worth, freedom, and ability as all other human beings. Unfortunately, ministers, theologians, and others in the African-American community were solely focused on racism that they were blind to the gender oppression of women. There was a different view of the doctrine of humanity when it came to African-American women. Women were viewed as weak and less capable than men solely on the basis of gender. Significantly, this was the same rationale (with gender replaced with race) that racists used to justify the oppression of African-Americans. Sexists and racists have the same oppressive belief in genetic inferiority. In the book, *Working with Black Youth: Opportunities for Christian Ministry*, in the chapter entitled "A Theological Framework," Jacquelyn Grant argues that the doctrine of humanity is of utmost importance for a full understanding of the meaning of God. It calls for humanity to adopt an ethic consistent with God as liberator rather than God as an unmerciful authoritarian. Grant asserts:

> The "who we are?" question has bearing upon who we say God is. The doctrine of humanity then is of utmost importance for comprehending the meaning of God, because human beings are responsible for theological concepts. . . . When theology gives support to a model of relationships based on domination and submission, the nature of humanity is severely distorted. . . . Women and other victims tend to be forced to the weak negative side of the social sexual dualism. Women are thereby perceived to be weak and submissive while men are viewed to be strong and dominant. In the realm of human interaction men function as God.[44]

The gender oppression of African-American women stems from a distorted view of humanity. African-American men assumed the dominant role in the African-American family, church, and community believing in a crude biblical and theological perception that women were created by God to be submissive and men to be dominant. This interpretation of the doctrine of humanity subject African-American women to the triple oppression of race, sex, and class. In his book, *The Prophethood of Black Believers*, J. Deotis Roberts states that in the oppression of African-American women, as in racism, the Bible, which can set us free, was used to enslave. The problem, according to Roberts, is biblical literalism; traditionally the Bible has been interpreted in ways that justify male domination. Biblical manipulation is an art that has been practiced by people all over the world, and both African-Americans and European-American racists are no exception. They set forth to find passages that they can interpret to mean specifically what they want to justify.[45] The doctrine of humanity has been distorted by racists and sexists to justify their oppressive agenda.

Female African-American theologians such as Jacquelyn Grant and Delores Williams have brought Black womanist theology to the forefront of theological discussion. In her book, *Sisters in the Wilderness: The Challenge of Womanist God-Talk*, Delores Williams lays out her vision for Black theology and the church. She wrote:

> The work of the African-American denominational churches' theologians, in consultation with the ministers and congregations, should be constantly to develop new principles for interpreting African-American people's history and the Bible principles taking seriously the faith-experience of African-American people rooted in Africa, in America and in resistance. It would no doubt be helpful for black religious scholars, along with ministers and congregations, to be involved constantly in the task of "revaluing value" so that black people can root out the African-American denominational churches the alien sexist, capitalist, class and color values black people have internalized in their process of becoming "Americanized" and "Christianized." Instruments for reevaluation should be shaped by a nonsexist, nonhomophobic, noncolorist, nonelitist Afrocentric perspective.[46]

Black womanist theologians share the objective of their male counterparts, to bring liberation to African Americans. However, Black womanist theologians believe that the full liberation of the African-American community cannot be attained without coming to terms with the oppression of women. Black male theologians such as James Cone, J. Deotis Roberts, Garth Baker-Fletcher, and Noel Erskine have in their writings and lectures urged the African-American church to take women seriously and to work in solidarity with them to bring healing and liberation to the African-American family, church, and community.

Until Black Womanist theology is granted due credit, the struggle for liberation will be incomplete and impaired. Baker-Fletcher asserts:

> one cannot truly claim allegiance to the African community's liberation or to Black churches unless one takes the entire history of Black women's experience as seriously

> as that of Black males. To stand for African-Americans is to stand with Black women, their tridimensional experience of oppression, their intellectual, economic, political, literary, and artistic achievements and disappointments. Taking Black women's experience as a source means to stand in solidarity with Black women.[47]

According to Baker-Fletcher solidarity with American-American females means commitment to the liberation struggle. Indeed, a consistent understanding of the doctrine of humanity with regard to women must be the starting point of solidarity. That is to say, the false myth of female inferiority must be replaced with the view that God created women as equals to men, and to be co-partners with them in God's work and in every aspect of human existence.

Two issues need to be more closely examined: First, Black Womanist theology is essential to Black theology; without it Black liberation theology would be incomplete. Second, the gender oppression of African-American women in the family, church, and community is rooted in a distorted understanding of the doctrine of humanity. Black Womanist theology is essential for the healing, liberation, and wholeness of the African-American community. Black Womanist theology's voice in the fight for the liberation of youths at risk must be heard; without its voice Black liberation theology will be incomplete. The voices of both Black Womanist theology and Black theology must become one voice and empower the church in its development of a plan of action to do ministry in a nihilistic culture and for the destruction of the African-American community's public enemy number one, the DCPC.

## The Black Church and Black Theology

The African-American church has struggled against racism informed by an informal and a formal Black theology. The latter is formulated in theological technique.

Informal Black theology is grounded in the faith tradition of the slave ancestors of African Americans. Informal Black theology originated in the midst of slavery and provided slaves with hope for freedom. This was the start of the faith tradition of African Americans. The slaves were suspicious of Christianity because it was the religion of their oppressors. In his book, *The Social Teaching of the Black Churches*, Peter J. Paris expounds on the dilemma in which the slaves found themselves when they accepted Christianity as their religion. He asserts:

> During the first century of their enslavement, blacks refused to accept Christianity, because they associated it wholly with the religion of their masters—a religion that viewed them as slaves by nature. Only after they had had the opportunity to reform the religion of their overseers did they accept Christianity.[48]

The reformation of Christianity was necessary for the slaves to establish a Christian faith tradition that would be authentic in their search for hope and meaning. An interpretation of the doctrine of humanity radically different from that of their masters was the departure point of informal Black theology. As mentioned above, the slave faith tradition empowered the slaves to adopt the faith position that God created them as human beings with the same values and freedoms as other human beings.

Historically, the African-American church has had a mission of radical involvement in the political, social, and economic struggles for liberation in an effort to reform the larger society. It devised strategies and methods it hoped would appeal to the religious conscience of European-American Christians, and result in the practice of racial justice from the perspective of the Christian love ethic.[49] The African-American church throughout its history has had to involve itself in every aspect of the African-American experience, and for centuries it was informal Black theology that empowered the church in initiatives for social transformation. J. Deotis Roberts writes that Gayraud Wilmore understood informal Black theology from an anthropological perspective. Wilmore asserts:

> It has been said that African American Theology began when the first slave wondered about a God whose followers kept people in chains while calling them "brothers and sisters." Frederick Douglas was a black theologian in this sense. Most people who think about the faith out of their experience of oppression and in the style and idiom of black Baptist, African Methodist and Pentecostal churches, or other churches influenced by those same traditions, are in this sense black or African American theologians.[50]

Wilmore's definition rightly implies that informal Black theology has shaped and formed many great advocates of liberation within this African-American religious tradition, and they are Black theologians.

It is out of this religious experience that the African-American church came to be recognized by its members and oppressors as an institution of influence. Paris expounds on the church's position of power in society when he argues,

> The black churches have constituted a place of power both within the black community and as the black community's representative in the white society. Their position of institutional primacy in the black community has enabled them to be the locus of racial social solidarity which, in turn, has comprised the basis of all cooperative activity aimed at racial advance . . . Consequently, they have been the major lobbying force of the black community for racial justice.[51]

The Civil Rights Movement of the 1960s led by Martin Luther King, Jr., is the best example of the church as a powerful institution in recent years. It was at this time that formal Black theology was born. The Civil Rights Movement began when Rosa Parks, a factory worker and a member of an African-American church, refused to give up her seat to a European-American man on a Montgomery bus on December 1, 1955. Martin Luther King, Jr., a formally trained theologian who had studied theology and ethics at Crozier Theological Seminary and Boston University, was chosen to be the President of the Montgomery Improvement Association, an organization started by local African-American churches. The churches in Montgomery organized a boycott against the city bus system which lasted for 389 days and ended with a victory that received national attention. The success of this boycott brought Martin Luther King, Jr., and the Civil Rights Movement much media coverage, and the African-American church gained national exposure and credibility as an institution of power in U.S. society.

Historically, the African-American church urged the participation of church members in the social and political struggles of the African-American community. However, King's national prominence as a pastor and a civil rights leader inspired the energetic participation of thousands of church members across the U.S. This reality caused many to fear the churches' ability to rally its followers and King's capacity to inspire the radical involvement of a great number of African Americans.

Finally, the African-American church must continue to advocate a Black theology that empowers it as an activist institution to work for spiritual, economic, social, and political change in the African-American community.

Black theology from pastoral care perspective will be discussed in chapter 5 in an effort to construct a model of ministry to destroy the DCPC.

# 4

# The DCPC and the African-American Community: A Model of Ministry for Healing

The Million Man March of October 16, 1995, and Canaan Baptist Church of Christ of Harlem, New York, are powerful models of ministry with a plan of action for healing and liberation in the African-American community. The present model of ministry will focus on healing the African-American youths who are at risk. These young persons, predominately male, have accepted an identity and lifestyle dominated by the Destructive Capitalistic Personality Complex or DCPC. The DCPC is the problem, and liberating the youths' from the DCPC is the challenge that this model of ministry will undertake.

## The Million Man March and the Spiritual Value of Self-Love

The Million Man March brought over one million African-American men to Washington, D.C., from areas across the U.S., as far west as Los Angeles and as far south as Miami. They came from Atlanta, Baltimore, Birmingham, Boston, Charlotte, Chicago, Cincinnati, Cleveland, Dallas, Detroit, Greensboro, Houston, Jackson, Jacksonville, Little Rock, Newark, St. Paul, St. Petersburg, Oakland, and Anchorage, Alaska. Why did they come? What did they wish to gain? These were the questions that were raised. The President of the United States, William Clinton, was not in Washington on that day, but he stated that he was pleased to see so many African-American men concerned about the plight of the African-American community. These men came to this march for spiritual renewal and to gain new inspiration to accept responsibility for healing, liberation, and the development of the African-American community. This large gathering of African-American men was unprecedented in U.S. history. The focus and function of this march as well as the widespread interest it generated hold enormous potential for the emergence of a major movement in the African-American community that will focus on widespread nihilism and the public enemy number one, the DCPC. Some of the participants in the Million Man March stated that they left Washington with an informed perspective on the African-American economic, social, and spiritual condition; they returned to their communities with a new focus and as different individuals. More importantly, they confirmed that this experience was spiritually enlightening; it gave them a new sense of dignity, self-love, self-respect, pride, family responsibility, and a sense of loyalty and commitment to the African-American struggle against oppression.

The Million Man March was a spiritual rally promoting spiritual values which are rooted in Malcolm X's notions of self-love.[52] The absence of self-love in African-American youths is the source of many problems, including crime, drug trafficking and abuse, violence, gang activity, the disproportionate amount of men in prison, unemployment and underemployment, low self-esteem, the lack of motivation to pursue an education, teenage pregnancy, misogyny, and rampant ignorance and hopelessness. The spiritual value of self-love is a deterrent to widespread nihilism. The DCPC is manifested when thousands of young men take up drug dealing without regard for the welfare of those to whom they sell. As discussed in chapter 2, the widespread use and selling of crack-cocaine in African-American communities across this nation has given rise to nihilism and the birth of the DCPC as we know it. Crack-cocaine was supplied to a huge number of people whose lives were destroyed; it is also responsible for bringing hundreds of young vulnerable at risk African-American men to a violent drug business. The absence of self-love's twin, love of others, resulted in these men's indifference to those their businesses affected and the development of the DCPC. The lack of self-love can lead to destructive behavior, and self-love is necessary before an individual can love others and understand the universal meaning of love, which affirms the sanctity of human life and the importance of the common good. In his book, *The Black Church in the African American Experience*, C. Eric Lincoln argues that the self-affirmation of African-Americans has had a positive effect on spiritual, social, and economic progress in the African-American community. He asserts:

> Since the civil rights period, the black revolution in consciousness has had a profound impact on the black community and on the larger society. Rev. Jesse Jackson's presidential campaigns in 1984 and 1988 and the election of thousands of black officials in the large urban areas and small towns are among the visible signs of this revolution manifested in the political sphere. Other signs included a large increase in the numbers of black students in colleges and graduate schools, an enlarged black middle class, and a period of creative ferment of black literary and intellectual talent reminiscent of the achievements of the Harlem Renaissance.[53]

Many other positive accomplishments in the African-American community are attributable to a strong sense of self-love and self-affirmation. The need for self-affirmation was advocated by Malcolm X. Garth Baker-Fletcher asserts, "Malcolm believed that self-respect had been systematically stripped away from American Blacks by the European-American system of racism."[54] The lack of self-love has dangerous existential consequences.

In his book, *Black Lies, White Lies: The Truth According to Tony Brown*, Tony Brown argues that African-Americans' negative perception of themselves as people of an inferior race defines their total outlook, which influences their spiritual and social behavior. He discusses an article published by the *Washington Post* entitled "Stereotype Within" that was about a sixth-grade public school class in Montgomery County, Maryland. The African-American students in the class were asked to speak on their impression of their race. A young girl articulated her impression of her race by stating, "everybody knows that Black people are bad. That's the way we are."[55] The tragedy, is that more than 90 percent of a class of 29 students believed that African-Americans were inferior. Brown states that the article went on to give a more detailed description of these students' impression of their race. He asserts:

> The *Washington Post* article outlined the tragic results of negative self-image and stereotypes among the young Black students. In general, they believed that: Blacks are poor and stay poor because they are dumber than Whites and Asians. Black kids who do their schoolwork and behave must want to be White. White kids who do poorly or dress cool want to be Black. Hispanic kids want to be Black because they aren't smart like Whites. Black people don't like to work hard. Blacks don't need to work hard because it won't matter in the end. Black people have to be bad so they can fight and defend themselves from other Blacks. Black men make women pregnant and leave. Black boys expect to die young and unnaturally. White people are smart and make money.[56]

Brown maintains that these young people were not defining themselves, but were defining their environment. He believes that this self-victimization has become a cultural legacy of many African Americans and is a great barrier to African-American progress.[57] Brown is right in his belief that self-love is necessary for liberation, and self-victimization is a barrier to African-American progress. Many of these same young people mentioned in the *Washington Post* article are already at risk for acquiring the DCPC. It is a negative perception of themselves that make them vulnerable to being misled by abusive drug dealers who take advantage of these youths. These often in their impressionable years are manipulated by drug dealers, and used to make a quick profit from drug dealing. The DCPC is a meanspirited and cold-hearted mindset with a total disregard for human worth and life. Many more youths will acquire the DCPC if drastic measures to boost self-love among African-American youths are not taken; it is the responsibility of Black theology and the Black church to respond to this problem.

In the book, *Working with Black Youth: Opportunities for Christian Ministry*, Janice Hale-Benson, in the chapter entitled "Psychosocial Experiences" states:

> The dire statistics on the compendium of problems of black youths are well known. How do black children endowed with innate equal childhood potential arrive at such a disadvantaged youth status? That question explores what in the schools reproduces failure in black children generation after generation. Schools do function as the major socializing institution in our society. Students who drop out, are pushed out, or are provided a diminished education are disconnected from a viable future. Other problems confronting black youth such as teen pregnancy, crime, drugs, and unemployment emanate from school failure. . . . Black children do not enter school disadvantaged. They emerge from school as disadvantaged youth.[58]

The Million Man March model of positive engagement and spiritual fellowship, grounded in self-love to promote responsibility to the struggle for liberation, is useful for the destruction of the DCPC. As indicated in chapter 3, the spiritual value of self-love was a part of the slave faith tradition. The Million Man March was an interfaith spiritual event that united African-American men to focus on the progress of the African-American community. The Million Man March model is a useful model for energizing a movement.

However, only men were invited by Louis Farrakhan, who asked women to stay at home, a statement that was oppressive to women. The uplift and participation of African-American women is equally important, particularly in light of the fact that they are the only parents in 70 percent of African-American homes.[59] Because of this exclusiveness, the Million Man March was incomplete and flawed.

The proposed model for use in African-American communities across the U.S. is a mini-model built on the same concept as the Million Man March. The same spiritual substance must be part of this model, but without the exclusiveness, calling for the full participation of women. This mini-model promotes the spiritual value of self-love with the same type of spiritual fellowship demonstrated in the original march, but among all African Americans rather than men only. Mini-marches would be organized by the participants of the October, 1995, march in their local communities. In fact, many of these communities have initiated campaigns to increase voter registration, assist in the adoption of African-American children, and discourage drugs and violence.

Finally, this mini-model calls for the radical involvement of the entire African-African community in teaching the spiritual value of self-love in an effort to destroy the DCPC. Teaching self-love throughout the nihilistic African-American communities in an intensive manner is one of the only real deterrents to keeping vulnerable youths at risk from becoming victimized by the DCPC. This sort of widespread educating of youths at risk on the self-pride and self-love that built African-American businesses, churches, schools, colleges, and institutions for social change is the type of movement now necessary to bring them out of this nightmare of crime, violence, ignorance, and self-destruction. The challenge for Black theology and the church is to engage youths at risk spiritually and intellectually in a new path where they will acquire the skills to find hope, and the spiritual substance to love themselves. The goal is for these youths at risk to become contributors to the cause of liberation rather than perpetrators of despair, statistics in prisons, victims of premature deaths, and young parents trapped in a life of despair. This type of movement will lay the foundation for liberation for this and future generations.

## The Canaan Baptist Church Model

Canaan Baptist Church sits in the middle of a poor neighborhood in Harlem, New York, but its approach to ministry has borne amazing results for the disadvantaged in that community. Wyatt Tee Walker, one of Martin Luther King, Jr.'s, followers, is creatively leading his nearly two thousand family congregation into the twenty-first century with a holistic approach to ministry that takes seriously the complexity of the spiritual, social, economic, and political issues related to the ongoing suffering of African-Americans. Although there are many other African-American congregations of different denominational persuasions that have demonstrated a firm commitment to the liberation of the disadvantaged, Canaan Baptist Church has been selected for the following reasons:

1. its location in a poor urban community;
2. its continuing successes in ministry;
3. its overall approach to ministry;
4. its methodology for youth empowerment.

At the National Conference on the Black Church and Community Economic Development held at the Harvard School of Divinity in April, 1994, Rev. Charles Adams explained why Wyatt Tee Walker was chosen to be the keynote speaker at that conference on community economic development.

> Wyatt Tee Walker was invited to articulate the aims and aspirations of the Harvard Conference on the economic structure and service of the Black Church because Canaan Baptist Church, of which he is the esteemed pastor, best represents that structure and that service.[60]

The Canaan Baptist Church model of ministry takes seriously every aspect of Christian discipleship to empower the church's ability to be a symbol of hope in disadvantaged Harlem. Walker believes that church disciples' tithes to the church is their commitment to the total church mission and to Christ's work of the liberation of the poor. The mission of the church is defined in Luke 4: 18–19, the text in which Jesus defined his mission. Walker understands this text from a Black theological perspective. That is, Jesus is salvation and liberation, and his focus was to liberate the poor and the oppressed. The point of departure of Jesus' mission was his promise of deliverance to the poor, which he declared in his reading of Isaiah 61:1–2 in a Nazareth synagogue as the theme of God's liberation of the poor. There are numerous other texts that support this Black theology tradition of liberation, but this one is particularly important to African-American pastors because Jesus declares that the promised deliverance of liberation was his primary focus and mission. Luke 4:18–19 is the statement of mission of Canaan Baptist Church in disadvantaged Harlem. The mission is a basic one of commitment to developing disciples and an outreach ministry that is designed to fight against oppression in every aspect of African-American life as a means to deliver the hope promised by Jesus.

### The Tithing Model: A Black Theology Perspective

Walker's total approach to ministry is grounded in the church's mission statement; from it he interprets a Christian principle of tithing as the foundation in which the church must operate as the agent for the spiritual cultivation of disciples, social engagement, the economic empowerment of the church and community, and the educational development of the youth. He argues:

> The Black family is under siege internally and externally; the unhampered flow of drugs into Black communities feeds on the despair induced largely by economic injustice and internally by the deterioration of the unit and self-inflected violence that kills Black males and children. All of this social havoc at this moment in history sits squarely on the front step of the African-American Church. This is precisely why the quantum leap on the tithing question is of such critical import.[61]

This model of ministry takes seriously the idea of self-help through economic development. According to Walker, the African-American church cannot fulfill its commitment to the poor without a strategic economic plan that will accumulate necessary resources to support ministry. He believes that the salvation of the race is in the hands of the African-American church and Christ, the liberator, and that the notion that an outside agency such as the U.S. government or a liberal entity will carry the torch of liberation is naive and is as destructive as the forces responsible for oppression. He affirms the theological position that the church is liberation and salvation because it is Christ in the world. Therefore, Canaan Baptist Church is Christ and the true hope of the poor in disadvantaged Harlem.

Canaan Baptist Church has emerged as a major religious, social, educational, political, and entrepreneurial institution in Harlem with the respect, dignity, and pride that success brings. The church's nearly two thousand family congregation earns an average annual salary just above 12,000 dollars. However, the tithing income is in excess of 1.2 million dollars and continues to grow. Walker attributes the fact that Canaan has 1,742 tithers to his teachings on tithing, the church's holistic approach to the ministry of liberation, the members' commitment to the vision of the church, and to Christ.[62] The Canaan Baptist Church complex is valued at 10 million dollars; it recently added a community center to the church complex that cost over 2.5 million dollars. The church owns and operates 437 affordable housing units in Central Harlem aimed at rebuilding that poor neighborhood; these housing units are valued in excess of 33 million dollars.[63] The Canaan Credit Union maintains a membership of more than 600 church members with more than 1.3 million dollars in assets. This financial institution carries life insurance for each member, sponsors a Christmas Club, and offers low-rate signature, automobile, and other loans as well as investments. Canaan Baptist Church operates several businesses which will be discussed later in the chapter.[64]

## The Political Model

Walker's political involvement is informed by Martin Luther King, Jr.'s, notion of radical involvement for social change. In a class for all new disciples of Canaan, political awareness, responsibility, and participation are an essential part of the spiritual orientation. It is taught that being a Christian carries with it the Christian responsibility of ministry to the poor, a biblical mandate to be taken seriously. Every Canaan disciple is encouraged to become a registered voter, and before each election, voter registration forms are made available at the church. Registering and voting are emphasized in the Canaan family.

## Pastoral Care Model

Canaan Baptist Church has a staff of four African-American pastors that manifests the scope of Black liberation theology. These ministers are all trained theologians and professional ministers. One is from the womanist Black theology tradition. According to Walker, she has been instrumental in teaching the church about gender, race, and class oppression from the black woman's perspective. The youth minister is a part of this staff of trained clergy. Additionally, the church has a staff of professionally trained counselors who provide family, personal, and financial counseling, and assist the pastoral staff with some spiritual counseling.

## Youth Ministry Model

Canaan Baptist Church has many important ministries that are informed by the Black theology tradition, but since the focus here is on the liberation the African American youths, the remaining discussion will focus on its model of ministry for youths. This model of ministry is a holistic strategic plan of action for the empowerment of young African-Americans. There are several ministries designed to liberate young African Americans and empower them to become productive disciples and successful Americans. They include:

**Cultural Enrichment**
This is a program of cultural enrichment for youths aged 10 to 25 that reaches into the Canaan and Harlem communities with activities related to African-

American history and culture, all manner of creative expression, resume-writing, job interviewing, and job etiquette. This program organizes trips to museums, plays, and movies, and maintains a reading club.

**Educational Enrichment**
Canaan has institutionalized a joint tutorial program for students in grades 2 to 8 with the Robert Francis Learning Center of Harlem. Services are offered by licensed teachers and experienced tutors who use a mixture of whole-group, small-group, and individualized instruction. The center teaches reading and mathematics for several hours each Saturday.

**Canaan's Intern Program**
Canaan provides professional training to young people to cultivate talent and develop skills by teaching them how to operate a business. The Canaan Catering Service, owned and operated by the church, provides internship opportunities to youths. They earn 10 dollars an hour, much more than the minimum wage, and learn the concept of business operation. Interns are also employed and trained to perform church administrative tasks such as the production of bulletins and programs, payroll preparation, and telephone reception. Interns develop skills in computer data entry, word processing, electronic switchboarding, and public relations.

**The Canaan Resource Center**
The center provides employment information to the Harlem community. Because the center advocates jobs for Harlem's disadvantaged, many businesses offer job opportunities and others outsource to local community institutions.

**Substance Abuse**
Canaan has several support groups for substance abusers. These groups are facilitated by Canaan disciples who are former substance abusers, and two Canaan disciples who are trained psychologists. These participants attempt continue to stay off crack, alcohol, and other drugs through these programs. These groups meet weekly and are dedicated to the healing process.

**Prison Ministry**
Canaan reaches into local prisons in an effort to guide young African Americans back to positive membership in American society. This ministry

provides a one-on-one mentor program to residents of a Bronx halfway house, maintains a weekly visitation program of spiritual enrichment, and sponsors a pen pal program between Canaan disciples and prisoners.[65]

Finally, Canaan Baptist Church is a viable religious institution with a holistic approach to ministry rooted in the Black theology tradition that is leading thousands of African Americans in a search for meaning. This author recommends this model of ministry to churches and mosques across the U.S. This model, along with the previously described model influenced by the Million Man March that calls for a collective ministry of African-American churches to promote the spiritual value of self-love, has the potential to promote the radical involvement of many in the fight to destroy the DCPC and nihilism. If churches across the country adopt the Canaan model of ministry, particularly youth ministry, the following will be possible:

1. After local churches use the Million Man March as a model to plant the seed of self-love, youths will then have many programs available to provide them spiritual nurturing and social, educational, professional, and economic assistance.
2. These youths will then become a part of the movement rather than a part of the problem.

# 5

# The Destructive Capitalistic Personality Complex and the Solution

What is needed now is a systematic plan of action for the destruction of the DCPC and the liberation of the African-American community. This plan of action utilizes the models discussed in chapter 4 as the structure for this Black theology movement. Additionally, this systematic plan of action will require the cooperation of many institutions in the African-American community and in society at large to play a vital role in a team effort. This endeavor must be carefully organized, led, and implemented by a strong African-American institution already working in this field that can use the Million Man March as its model. This writer advocates the National Committee of Black Christians as that organization because of its diverse makeup of theologians, scholars, ministers, and community activists. Additionally, the model of the Million Man March must be a key part of this team effort in order to expand the interest inspired by the Million Man March, with the mini-model in local communities across the U.S. Some of the ideas and suggestions of Deborah Prothrow-Stith and Michaele Weissman stated in *Deadly Consequences* are with much merit and will be adopted. Michael Eric Dyson's argument presented in his book, *Reflecting Black: African-American Cultural Criticism*, will be helpful in finding a solution to the drug problem.

The problems of the DCPC and nihilism are complex and will be difficult to resolve. There are many components of suffering and destruction connected to this ongoing cycle of oppression which have made it difficult for community activists and Black theology to determine which component of this despair is most deadly and must be dealt with first. An effective movement must resist the traditional strategy of fighting racism and being preoccupied with racism. The spiritual energy of the African-American community will not be effectively used this way. Racism at large is too big and vague a target; though, fighting it is somewhat necessary for all of society, total focus on it by the African-American community will not be feasible to achieve concrete results within a certain amount of time. Nor will its demise resolve some of the other issues that African-Americans must face for liberation to become a reality. In fact, racism finds life in the heart, which makes it a spiritual problem and issue for the person consumed by its evilness. African-Americans with God's direction and help will maintain control only over their own spirituality. Human beings are responsible for their choices, and whether one is a racist, a saint, or an ethnically upright and good person, being a racist will be contingent upon one's own spiritual choices. African-Americans must never again accept full spiritual or moral responsibility to solely rid our society of its deeply seated racist beliefs; society as a whole is morally responsible for the shape and transformation of its moral and spiritual culture. It is time for the African-American community to spend its spiritual energy and resources focused on liberation from a spiritual healing and economic development perspective. Fighting the DCPC, a clearly defined target, must be the first goal of a movement today.

A vast number of young African Americans grow up disadvantaged by poverty, substandard education, and prejudice, and eventually perceive the drug business as the only means to self-esteem and success. Instead of finding true meaning and hope, they acquire the DCPC. The nihilistic and materialistic culture in which they live leaves them vulnerable enough to want to risk their lives in a lifestyle of crime and violence. When these young persons decide to acquire the destructive values of the DCPC, material success at any cost, they lose regard for the sanctity of human life. The DCPC qualifies as a self-destructive force because it prevents progress in the African-American community through certain immoral habits of African American youths. In deed, the self-destructive behavior patterns that are so ubiquitous among African American youths are produced in them by the public enemy number one, the DCPC. These young people surrender to the DCPC, and it ends their hope and unleashes forces in the African-American community that significantly scale-down progress and liberation.

The military theory of fighting small wars until one is capable of winning the big war is the strategy that Black theology in the U.S. must adopt. After the Vietnam War, military strategists concurred that thereafter, before the U.S. committed troops to a military engagement, it must have a clearly defined, focused, and feasible goal. The more feasible goal of fighting the DCPC must be the initial goal of a movement for the liberation of the African-American youths. It is a realistic way to attack the larger issue of racism.

Furthermore, the systematic plan of action must include every aspect of society that is currently a part of the problem and turn them into a part of the solution. The church, African-American institutions, political institutions, law enforcement institutions, and educational institutions must be addressed by the plan of action. They will each be mentioned, but some in more detail. Each step of this plan of action will include the following strategies.

## Step 1: Black Theology

The argument as presented in the book is that Black theology in any culture cannot be effective when it does not have a clear, focused, limited, and feasible goal and when it spreads itself too thin. In order for Black theology to be effective it must have a clearly defined vision focusing on a specific target, and a function at the grassroots level. The function is the action, which is taken by the church, but without a clearly defined vision focusing on a specific target, the plan of action will fail. Black theology in the United States did not gain the kind of grassroots support necessary to ignite a movement. Furthermore, it is important to mention that Cone's Black theology was rejected by the African-American Church in the United States. Cone cannot be blamed for the failure of a movement to emerge at the grassroots. Nevertheless, Cone's Black theology has been quite helpful to the African-American Church; it set forth to take the Black Liberation movement of the 1950s and 1960s a step further between the 1970s and 1990s. South African Black theologians constructed a South African Black theology from James Cone's Black theology of Liberation. Additionally, they used the term *Black Theology*, which was coined in the United States. Basil Moore credits Cone's work, *A Black Theology of Liberation*,[66] for its contribution to the development of a Black liberation theology in South Africa.

As mentioned above, Black theology in South Africa emerged with a movement because it focused on apartheid, which it identified as the public enemy number one. Not only were Black South Africans motivated to fight apartheid, but people and governments around the world supported and adopted South African Black theology vision, and its call for the destruction apartheid. This is clearly not a suggestion that everyone in the world community participated in this liberation effort. However, African Americans, some economic institutions, churches around the world, components of the world media, and certain governments believed that apartheid was evil and they sided with the protestors and not the South African government. They provided support of the vision of the South African Black theology movement through economic boycotts and moral critiques of apartheid in speeches, articles, sermons, books, and various other means. This movement was grounded in the courage and faith of the people to fight for justice and freedom. There were powerful spiritual and political dynamics of the South African Black theology and political liberation movements that led to the dismantling of apartheid. The African National Congress (ANC) provided the political vision and focus, and the Black theology movement educated, inspired, and motivated the masses. They both harmonized to make the fight one meaningful spiritual and political struggle. The success of this movement led to the establishment of a new government, a new constitution, and the destruction of apartheid. Many church leaders were members of the ANC and many ANC followers and leaders were also members of the Black church. However, the ANC had been in place as a major institution to be reckoned with for several decades before Black theology emerged in South Africa as a movement. The ANC had established its political philosophy and methodology to fight against apartheid, and continued to develop as an organization, improving its philosophy and methodology. The ANC grew massively during the years after the Black theology movement intensified at the grass roots. The ANC was the political machine behind the success of the impassioned fight that defeated apartheid. In fact, the ANC was already in place before South African Black theology spiritually awakened the Black masses; it was already organized to provide the political vision and muscle for the revolution. Indeed, it also had the clout to attract white liberals in South Africa, and to rally the support of countries, institutions, and individuals around the world.

Black theology in the U.S. has the substance, but has not championed a vision that focuses on a sole target. In the U.S., Black theology has focused on racism at large rather than identifying a concrete target and promoting it as the African-American community's public enemy number one. This has resulted in the lack of motivation and support of people to attack such a poorly defined enemy. However, if the enemy is identified, like this author identifies the DCPC, it is easier for people to grasp the necessity of a movement and be motivated to join it. The DCPC, as public enemy number one, would give U.S. Black theology the crucial clarity.

The first step of the plan of action calls for U.S. Black theology to establish a vision, a focus, and a function to wage a movement against the DCPC and its twin, nihilism.

## Step 2: Church and Community Model

The Million Man March was attended by 1.2 million African Americans who came from communities all over the nation. This response indicates a movement that is waiting to be born. The Million Man March lacked vision because it was not inclusive of women, but had the focus, the spiritual value of self-love. The function must expand to churches in local communities.

As mentioned above, this strategic plan of action influenced by the Million Man March needs an African-American organization to implement this model in local communities as the key initial step. The National Committee of Black Christians (NCBC) is the idea organization for realizing implementation. The movement's goal will be to destroy the DCPC with the help of the African-American church. The function of this model has two components.

The first function is the NCBC's implementation of the Million Man March model in local communities across the U.S.; this model is designed to bring churches and mosques together to teach the spiritual value of self-love. The NCBC would organize quarterly spiritual rallies in areas where nihilism is rampant. With the guidance of local church leaders these rallies will have the same substance the 1995 Washington march had. This strategic plan of action calls for the teaching of self-love by churches and mosques in local communities in a radically involved manner. The Million Man March's message of self-love captivated its participants because it made a profound connection with the destruction of the family, crime, the drug crisis, violence, and gang activity. The participants pledged love to themselves, to each other, and to all African-American men. They promised not to disrespect African-American women and children. They pledged to be loyal to the African-American struggle for liberation. They pledged to join the struggle for hope in their local communities. They pledged to love themselves by not abusing their bodies, souls, and minds with lethal substances. This march inspired people to adopt the spiritual value of self-love.

African-American women make up the overwhelming majority of African-American churches' membership. Delores Williams maintains that if African-American women left, the African-American church would cease to exist.[67] African-American men make up a minority of African-American churches' membership, but the Million Man March attracted more than one million of them. This model suggests that these types of spiritual rallies are what is needed to inspire people in African-American communities across the U.S., and that it is the NCBC that has the potential to set this strategic plan of action into motion. These marches in local communities will originate at the grassroots level and soon grow into a national movement.

The second function of this model is the promotion of the Canaan Baptist Church model. The next step for the NCBC is to publicize the Canaan Baptist Church model of ministry to other African-American churches in an effort to empower them to become major religious, social, and economic institutions. Sharing a common model and vision will generate unity among and within churches, and congregations will subsequently grow as Canaan did in Harlem. The Canaan model takes ministering to the disadvantaged seriously: Canaan's ministries focus on the spiritual, social, economic, educational, professional, and personal needs of Harlem's disadvantaged. The church has developed into a major religious and economic institution in Harlem. Canaan's success is attributable to, first, its teachings on tithing; second, its teaching that true discipleship brings with it a commitment and responsibility to God and to the disadvantaged that calls for responsible citizenship, community loyalty, and church commitment; third, its many ministries and programs are for the uplift of African-American life. The Canaan Baptist Church is a model for other churches to follow; it provides the African-American community with more resources in the fight against oppression and recognizes the value of self-love and self-help. The pastor of Canaan, Wyatt Tee Walker, often says the Black church must free its people from oppression because no government, outside agency, or liberal organization of goodwill can do it. The African-American church is the primary institution that can do this.

## Step 3: The Drug Problem

The DCPC is manifested in the drug problem in the African-American community. Self-love is a determining factor in whether a youth will or will not acquire the DCPC. Young people in search of meaning, but disadvantaged by the consequences of racism, are vulnerable to the DCPC. When poverty, substandard education, and prejudice hamper their job prospects, the drug business appears to be the only feasible path to material success and a sense of self-worth. In his book, *Reflecting Black: African-American Cultural Criticism*, Michael Eric Dyson argues that

> when traditional avenues for the realization of personal growth, esteem, and self-worth, usually gained through employment and career opportunities, have been closed, young black men find gangs a powerful alternative. Gangs also offer

> immediate material gratification through a powerful and lucrative underground economy.[68]

Profits from the crack business has enabled gangs to become powerful, organized, and armed organizations. For many young African Americans, becoming a crack dealer is the way to achieve material success and a sense of worth. Michael Eric Dyson suggests why thousands of young African-Americans get involved in the drug culture, and how it is devastating the African-American community. He asserts:

> One of the more devastating developments in inner-city communities is the presence of drugs and the criminal activity associated with their production, marketing, and consumption. Through the escalation of the use of the rocklike form of cocaine known as *crack* and intensified related gang activity, young black men are involved in a vicious subculture of crime. This subculture is sustained by two potent attractions: The personal acceptance and affirmation gangs offer and the possibility of enormous economic reward.[69]

The subject of how to wage an effective war against drugs has been much debated. In his book, *Empower the People*, Theodore Walker, Jr., explains:

> Moreover, both liberal and conservative public policy analysts agree that drug-related activity, aside from being a crime in itself, contributes to the increase of other criminal activity. To be sure, it is now widely conceived that the largest part of war against crime should consist of war against drugs, and also that both public and private sectors, including the work place, should join this war.[70]

However, the African-American community must become proactive and give assistance to policy makers in the effort to finally eliminate drugs from its community. Too much is at stake for the African-American community to fail to give meaningful assistance to help policy makers and law enforcement officials develop and implement a strategy to fight drugs with its involvement and input. In the past, African Americans have been the victims of policies that were supposed to help them. Walker argues:

> Clearly, Afro-America shares concern with, and suffers greatly from, abusive drug use and criminal activity. However, from our perspective it appears that many current and impending versions of warring against drugs and crime amount to war against black and colored people. Our experience of war on drugs and crime has been one of increased suffering and oppression.[71]

The African-American church must help lead the war against drugs in its own communities through its involvement with local law enforcement agencies; it must monitor law enforcement agencies' activities and work with them to prevent crime among youths at risk. With the recent allegations against two of the nation's largest police departments, the New York City Police Department (NYPD) and the Los Angeles Police Department (LAPD), a cooperative working relationship between law enforcement agencies and the African-American community is imperative. The New York Police Department came under scrutiny when Abner Louima, a Hatian-American, was sexually brutalized by a police officer with a broomstick in a Brooklyn precinct house. Furthermore, an unarmed West African student, Amadou Diallo, was killed in the foyer of his apartment building in Bronx, New York. In addition, Patrick Dorismond, an off-duty security guard, was killed in March, 2000, after he grew angry at undercover officers who tried to buy drugs from him; no drugs or other contraband were found on him. Josh Getlin, staff writer for the *Los Angeles Times,* writes, "the demands for change have escalated recently as plainclothes officers fatally shot two unarmed black men in separate incidents after physical struggles with them."[72] African-American community leaders in New York City called for a U.S. Justice Department investigation of the death of Diallo. These leaders have registered serious concern about unfair racial profiling of American Americans and Latinos. According to the March 20, 2000, issue of the *Los Angeles Times,* four blocks from where Diallo was killed, Malcolm Ferguson, a suspected drug dealer, was killed by NYPD police officers. Community leaders responded to this March, 2000, killing with outrage and called for the U.S. Department of Justice to investigate.

The Los Angeles Police Department's Rampart Division scandal has generated national attention. There are allegations that some LAPD police officers planted and tampered with evidence in numerous cases in order to obtain a conviction. Community leaders in Los Angeles are outraged, and these matters are under investigation by Los Angeles city and county officials. In order to make policing effective in minority communities, law enforcement agencies need the assistance of communities. This will be the start in an effort to repair the tense relations between the police and minorities and the perception that they are prejudiced and abusive. This type of cooperative effort will be a crime prevention measure. It is important for these communities to be actively involved in police practices for crime prevention and human rights reasons.

The question of whether police departments are practicing racial profiling and other overly aggressive tactics with African-Americans is now being examined. There has been a historic distrust of the police in the African-American community. The incidents involving the LAPD and NYPD and negative perceptions further complicate the teaching of moral discipline to youths at risk. Reports of racial profiling perpetuate fear in African-Americans. This produces new spiritual challenges for the African-American community. Intensive work in the area of crime prevention will help keep youths at risk from acquiring the DCPC. African-American churches and mosques must do the following: (1) collective efforts among churches and mosques to establish drug rehabilitation clinics; these churches must explore the possibility of obtaining federal matching funds; (2) establish pastoral care programs focused on healing substance abusers in local communities across the nation; (3) religious institutions with drug rehabilitation clinics and pastoral care programs for substance abusers must share resources with other institutions that do not have clinics and programs; (4) have former drug dealers and abusers participate in a drug prevention program by speaking at schools, parks, recreational facilities, and other places where young people congregate.

The Canaan ministry model for pastoral care must be promoted by the NCBC in an effort to help other churches develop a pastoral care model of ministry and get involved in ministering to the needs of drug abusers. The NCBC must solicit and benefit from the knowledge and expertise of theologians, ministers, activists, and scholars. Edward Wimberly and Richard Cobble are two such people. Edward Wimberly has written extensively on the subject of pastoral care in the Black church, and his work has been helpful to African-American pastors.[73] Wimberly's ideas must be utilized by the NCBC in this strategic plan of action. Additionally, Richard Cobble, Assistant Pastor at Ebenezer Baptist Church in Atlanta, Georgia, and the founder of Agape House, a drug rehabilitation clinic in Atlanta, is extremely knowledgeable on the subject of substance addiction. Cobble is a Black theologian whose clinical approach has a spiritual emphasis. Agape House has rehabilitated and helped hundreds of crack addicts become productive citizens in their communities. Agape house is a drug clinic that deserves to be adopted as a model by African-American communities. Cobble specializes in substance abuse treatment and, in his doctoral dissertation, made a thorough and insightful examination of holistic church initiatives.[74] Cobble could serve as the NCBC's National Field Representative. There are numerous other African-American churches across the U.S. with drug clinics whose ministry models, experience, and expertise may be edifying.

### Step 4: Community Policing

Some of the methods law enforcement agencies use to police under-class communities have generated resentment and alienation rather than positive feelings and cooperation. Police officers patrol these communities from their cars. Foot patrolling allows officers to interface with community people in a more intimate and friendly way. In their book, *Deadly Consequences*, Deborah Prothrow-Stith and Michaele Weissman argue in favor of foot patrol for less antagonistic community relations. She asserts, "new brand of policing that advocates the return of foot patrol interests me very much—not only as a tactic for improving police community relations,but also as method of combating crime."[75] According to Prothrow-Stith and Weissman, the method of policing that is in use in most cities has failed because it is motivated by statistics, that is, the number of arrests made. Ironically, crime has increased.[76] Prothrow-Stith and Weissman advocate a preventive plan that targets areas where crime is more likely to occur by making infrastructural changes. For example, if night after night drug dealers gather on a darkened playground, instead of arresting them only to witness them released a few hours later, install high density lights, thus making the area too bright and less attractive for business transactions.[77] This is not to suggest that drug dealers not be pursued, but that law enforcement must develop preventive measures as a deterrent to crime.

The radical involvement of African Americans in the formation of policing policies is necessary for constructive, rather than antagonistic, law enforcement. The African-American community must take the initiative to make community policing a part of the solution rather than a part of the problem.

### Step 5: The Political Strategy

This plan of action is centered around the radical involvement of African-American churches in their local communities for spiritual growth, economic development, and community improvement at all levels from the perspective of self-love and self-help. Historically, the African-American church has aggressively pursued a political agenda as a means to resolve many of its ills. This political activity included participating in the Civil Rights Movement, promoting voter registration and voting, educating people on political issues and candidates, and endorsing opposing certain candidates for public office. In spite of this, a vast number of African-Americans remain politically apathetic. In his book, *The Black Church in the African American Experience*, C. Eric Lincoln says that many African Americans are uninspired by the political system itself. He asserts:

> our research data on the seven mainline black denominations, which represent more than 80 percent of all black Christians, indicate that only 8.4 percent of the clergy supported the view of noninvolvement in such problems. . . . the vast majority (91.6 percent) of black clergy nationwide advocated church involvement in social and political issues. However, these results are important in debunking the myth that religious alienation is the cause for the political alienation of large numbers of black people from the electoral process. The causes for the alienation are to be found in the political system itself, and the continuing dilemma of racism in a society which wants to be perceived as democratic and under God.[78]

This plan of action calls for an intensified grassroots involvement at the local level. Historically, local political involvement has brought about advances in civil rights. Local communities must focus on improving educational institutions and constructive programs that channel young people's energy to positive paths.

This plan of action employing the two models previously mentioned calls for local churches and mosques to work collectively with a clearly defined goal. The focus is the battle against the DCPC, but the local organizations must include political action among its tools. Educational institutions have an essential role in shaping the spiritual, emotional, and mental development of African-American youths, and it is the educational institutions that require primary attention. Its reform will be facilitated by political policy, and African Americans must become proactive and take ownership of the school system they support with their tax dollars.

## Conclusion

Several steps are presented in this systematic plan of action to attack the public enemy number one of the African-American community, the Destructive Capitalistic Personality Complex (DCPC). South African Black theology developed a motivated movement and set the stage for the destruction of apartheid, which it identified as its primary enemy. South African Black theology was relevant in the daily lives of the oppressed in South Africa because it was a powerful weapon against the oppressive forces. Black theology in South Africa had the following elements: first, a vision that the people shared; second, a focus on a sole public enemy; third, a clearly defined function to destroy that enemy. As has been argued in the preceding chapters, Black theology in the U.S. needs to develop a movement at the grassroots level to combat the DCPC. This systematic plan of action will teach the spiritual value of self-love throughout disadvantaged African-American communities using two models. The Million Man March mini-model serves as the methodology to teach the spiritual value of self-love. The second model is the Canaan Baptist Church ministry model, which has a view to make African-American churches emerge as powerful social, economic, and educational institutions for the empowerment of the disadvantaged in local communities across the nation and for the destruction of the DCPC. This plan of action has proposed a specific strategy informed by Black theology and to be implemented by an African-American institution, the NCBC.

Historically, African-American youths have led the struggle against racism. The Civil Rights Movement of the 1950s and 1960s was spearheaded by young people such as the 25-year-old Martin Luther King, Jr., and the 28-year-old Ralph Abernathy. Throughout history, it has been young people who have had the idealism, vision, passion, and energy to challenge the establishment. Christianity entered the world as a youth movement. Jesus was a young man of 30 when he started his ministry. His disciples were in their early 20s when they went out to follow him. The beginning of Christianity is actually the story of twelve young people working to transform a sinful world.

This book is not merely about saving youths; the future is in their hands, and African Americans must fight against oppression in each generation.

# 6

# Youths at Risk and Spiritual Healing

The primary challenge for the African-American community in the coming years will be to cultivate a spirituality from Black theology that will teach practical moral principles in an effort to change self-destructive behavior patterns. These self-destructive patterns have become forces that hinder social and economic transformation. This book proposes spiritual principles that will give youths at risk the moral discipline to move from self-destruction to self-realization, and from nonparticipation to total involvement in the struggle for community development. When youths at risk discover a deep spiritual awareness and inner healing the spread of nihilism will decrease and community solidarity and social transformation will be possible. This will allow Black theology to be introduced to African-American youths in a spiritually meaningful and practical way. This approach will change Black theology from merely being a theological voice against oppression to a feasible plan that will equip African Americans with the spiritual substance to bring spiritual and social liberation to the African-American community. Only a spiritual revolution of this magnitude will realize the practical application necessary for the liberation of African Americans in the coming years.

The time has come for Black theology to rise to the occasion and become a practical means to teach youths at risk. Black theologians must broaden the scope of the purpose and meaning of Black theology into the practical experience of the African-American community. It must mature from being a prophetic voice that critiques the effects of racism to include strategies for teaching practical spiritual principles for African Americans. There is an urgency to equip youths at risk with the moral values that will liberate them from behavior patterns that are destroying their lives and perpetuating self-imposed despair. The validity of the prophetic meaning of the black struggle from the perspective of Christ has been firmly established in theology. Black theology gave intellectual and spiritual wisdom in interpreting black oppression. Black theology has been eye-opening and necessary, and aided the goal of liberation. Dr. James Cone, a professor of Systematic Theology at Union Seminary, made seminal and substantive contributions. Cone provided all

Christian traditions with a serious and credible critique of theology, especially those traditions that did not view or understand God as liberator. However, the critique must expand to community action. The challenge for practitioners of Black theology, theologians, ministers, and activists will be to bring Christ to the midst of the despair in the African-American experience through practical applications. A discourse that will focus on the development of spiritual principles in youths at risk is necessary. This discourse must occur in the Black church, but it must also happen in educational and social institutions and have total community involvement. This type of discourse will facilitate teaching youths at risk the practical application of the spiritual principles of Black theology. The wisdom of Cone and other Black theologians must now be applied to empower youths at risk with the spiritual substance and moral discipline to overcome the DCPC. A practical, strategic plan of this nature will have widespread implications on the ongoing struggle for spiritual transformation. The details of this discourse will be discussed in the final chapter.

This plan will capitalize on the spiritual energy and willpower that are a part of the spiritual tradition and souls of African-Americans since they first arrived in the U.S. They are responsible for bringing African Americans from 1502 to the present. In 1502 an untold number of Africans were first brought to what is now U.S. shores by early European settlers to be enslaved. However, they killed many of these Europeans and escaped. Oral tradition claims that they lived with and intermarried with Native Americans. This plan will set forth to refocus and build upon this energy and willpower in the African-American community; it will cultivate spiritual awareness in order to foster individual moral responsibility and produce community solidarity. The positive implications will end the self-destructive cycles of nihilism that have intensified and spread rapidly throughout the African-American community in the past thirty or more years. The DCPC can be overcome when these youths gain spiritual awareness informed by the Black theology tradition. In order for Black theology to become more applicable in the struggle against oppression, it must include a plan of action with a specific focus.

The plan is a simple one. It merely calls for the harnessing of the spiritual energy of the movements of the 1950s, 1960s, and 1970s in the African-American community. The substance at the core of this plan is based on several spiritual principles that are discussed thoroughly in the next chapter.

This spiritual energy will be directed to the development of these principles to confront and ultimately systematically destroy the DCPC. This spiritual energy that rallied the black community together in past movements no longer exists at the same intensified level. Traditional Black Power rhetoric about the power of racism upon the Black experience was largely responsible for bringing the masses together, the success of the civil rights movement, and the heightened consciousness of some European Americans. The first thing that the Black Power Movement did was to improve the awareness of African Americans through cultural identification and positive reinforcement. The Black Power Movement had a positive message about blackness. It held that blackness was beautiful and black people intelligent, spiritual, and important to U.S. culture. It promoted ethnic pride; it taught black people about the African Diaspora in the U.S., and that only a strong determined people could fight for justice in the midst of overwhelming oppression and still have their faith and a sense of their heritage. Second, it held that obtaining a good education and gaining self-reliance were both important components of black liberation. King's nonviolent direct action was more acceptable to many than the ideology of the Black Power Movement or Malcolm X's call to use any means necessary. King's approach appeared to be the best alternative to many and appealed to more European Americans. Blaming racism solely for the plight of African Americans has lost credibility. Since integration, a large number of African Americans have come to believe that racism cannot hold back individual determination, and perhaps this is the key reason for the decreased level of participation in the struggle for liberation. Some African Americans shifted their focus from community liberation to personal advancement. This shift has proven to be costly to common progress. There was less participation in the struggle for social change and more pursuit of personal material gain. A large number of talented persons focused on individual financial progress rather than community progress. This has led to the wane of the community power that had succeeded in sustaining African-Americans from slavery to Jim Crow, and from Jim Crow to the passage of the civil rights acts of the 1960s.

This phenomenon hurt the development of leadership in the African-American community. There was a loss in vision and community identity. Most devastating is that a large number of the less fortunate and those who remained in African-American neighborhoods after many accomplished African Americans left turned to immoral leadership. Individual material gain became the top priority of the less fortunate as well, but it was often sought through unethical means and led to what I call the DCPC.

This was a major paradigm shift that devastated leadership development and unity. At the same time, there was also a paradigm shift in U.S. social policy, specifically monitoring individual African Americans' progress to measure the alleviation of racism. This paradigm shift in U.S. domestic policy stimulated the African-American community to promote assimilation into the dominant culture. The country assessed individuals' personal progress as a means to measure African-American progress. This was a paradigm shift that contributed to the demise of essential institutions in the African-American community. African Americans began to see other African Americans prosper financially, move into more expensive neighborhoods, and send their children to better schools. This, in turn, has led even more individuals to start focusing on personal rather than community advancement. Unfortunately, too many of these individuals, because of lack of opportunities, interest in education and legitimate work, or talent or greed, turned to immoral means to obtain success, acquiring the DCPC.

The new policy changed the way African-American progress was assessed. This mechanism was implemented to monitor African-American progress to determine whether racism was decreasing in U.S. society. To protect their organizations from discrimination lawsuits many businesses and governmental institutions also gathered statistical data. Numbers were used to assess racism. This method was used by civil rights organizations as well. As more individuals prospered the emphasis changed from community liberation to individual progress. The struggle for liberation that was once advocated by a whole community had given way to the pursuit of individual advancement. The DCPC emerged as a consequence of this shift. Those left behind acquired the same desire for material gain, but acquired the DCPC as their means.

Middle-class African Americans in large numbers realized professional and economic gain due to progress in civil rights. The paradigm shift had a positive as well as a negative impact upon U.S. society. The movements of the 1960s and the actions of President Lyndon B. Johnson's administration spurred this change. The Civil Rights Act of 1964 and the Voting Rights Act of 1965 were passed. Progress against racism became interpreted as individual, rather than community, advancement. During this period, the second paradigm shift occurred; middle-class African Americans advanced and forgot about the community cause. The middle-class turned their focus away from community liberation to their own self-liberation. Affirmative action opened doors of opportunity as universities admitted and awarded financial aid to African-Americans. Segregated communities integrated. It seemed that the doors of opportunity were finally opened by the Civil Rights Movement and that the fight for justice was over. However, we now know that a great number of poor persons were not prepared to take advantage of these opportunities in this new social reality. These two paradigm shifts gave rise to a spiritual crisis that has lasted for several decades. The poor and uneducated were left behind without leadership and have been shaped in communities plagued by widespread nihilism.

The paradigm shifts helped the middle-class; many of them assimilated into mainstream society and found professional achievement and financial advancement. But too many more fell deeper into despair and poverty. The noted African-American sociologist, William Julius Wilson, in his book *The Truly Disadvantaged* argues that the black flight to white neighborhoods in the 1960s and 1970s resulted in a drain of talent and resources. Integration has profoundly harmed the African-American community at large. It depleted the African-American community of spiritual, social, and economic resources that had been provided by accomplished middle-class professionals, entrepreneurs, and role models. The middle-class had provided role models and a process of human development for the poor. The poor and uneducated were left to fend for themselves. They have become a growing underclass in nihilistic communities across the nation today. The black flight destroyed community solidarity and led to the destruction of important institutions which had been the foundation that provided an ongoing process of human development. Integration led to the flight of talented people who had served as leaders.[79] Leadership in human development was essential for the disadvantaged to acquire inspiration and practical knowledge. In the African-American experience the ethos of communal cooperation and participation in society is crucial because community members rely upon each other to survive oppression. However, when the people of the community are separated from each other the customs that gave them order, power, and solidarity will disappear, and hopelessness and disorder will emerge. Afrocentrism served as a mechanism to restore and maintain order; it produces a culture of community identification and involvement. The individual finds identity and stability from the community. Afrocentrism leads the community to shape the individual. In other worldviews, community identity is secondary to individualism. African Americans needed and depended upon each other and were too vulnerable for massive assimilation when it occurred. Consequently, the community suffered a traumatic setback after integration. The disadvantaged needed their educated, middle-class brethren for human development. Human development involves keeping a strong spiritual, moral, and progressive African community in place to help shape all African-Americans in the Afrocentric tradition. These paradigm shifts brought about poverty and despair that have grown into widespread nihilism. Youths at risk are the product of this social despair. Doubtlessly, before these shifts there were poverty and despair. However, these paradigm shifts destroyed the community unity that stabilized communities and had the potential to effect meaningful social change. The challenge is to introduce this rich spiritual tradition to our youths at risk and cultivate in them the moral values of their ancestors. Many youths never had the opportunity to learn how important and useful their spiritual heritage is in their self-realization. What once created community unity was replaced with capitalistic individualism. African-Americans have directed their spiritual energy on personal goals rather than the common good. This was not the case with the spiritual energy that sustained the slaves and gave power to the movements of Martin Luther King, Jr., Malcolm X, and the black power advocates of the 1960s and 1970s. I advocate teaching youths at risk ten spiritual principles that will build community rather than destroy it. Many African-Americans have become successful due to integration and assimilation, but many more have joined the ranks of the underclass.

Some argue that today there is enough opportunity for every citizen to rise from poverty and despair if they have the determination. This position ignores the historical reality that progress has come about in the African-American community through communal efforts. Therefore, community solidarity and spiritual healing are crucial in the fight against nihilism and the DCPC. Our energy must now be used more wisely and constructively because circumstances have changed in the U.S. Even affirmative action has suffered setbacks. The arguments blaming racism for many of the problems in the African-American community have lost acceptance among influential people, including policy makers. Racism certainly plays an important role in the spread of nihilism in the African-American community. Indeed, racism is key to understanding the cause of nihilism; it is the evil that made the African Diaspora a historical reality in the U.S. However, it is simply too large a target and to think that society can miraculously transcend it is simply naïve.

African Americans are not solely responsible for ending racism and must never again feel that they must assume the entire burden. The entire society is responsible for eliminating racism. Racism is infinite and finds life in the personality. Therefore, African Americans cannot be expected to take the responsibility for changing a racist attitude; the responsibility lies with the individual to allow Jesus' message of love to bring healing. The reality is, there are still racists in the church in spite of the love principle of Christ. At the core of liberation is economic self-reliance. Economic power is something that is created or taken. "Economic power" here means the kind that is created through moral means. Material gain is the objective of youths with the DCPC, and they view crime as their only means to reach it. To stop this destructive capitalistic behavior requires spiritual development. Even Malcolm X at one time suffered from the DCPC, and his faith redirected and reshaped his life with a new moral compass. Furthermore, even though racism has adversely affected African-Americans' spiritual and social reality they must hold themselves accountable for self-destructive beliefs and behavior patterns. It is one thing to be harmed by racism, but it is another to destroy oneself. When one works against oneself one must take responsibility and not blame racism solely for self-destructive behavior tendencies. African Americans must harness their spiritual power to reach healing and social transformation even if racism is at work. We must spend our energy on restoring moral character and discipline, and the starting point is with African-American youths at risk who are being shaped by a nihilistic culture that the African-American community did not solely create, but is the caretaker that must end it.

The African-American community's energy must now become grounded in a radical spirituality rooted in the Black theology perspective in order to establish a moral foundation for youths at risk, which must be the agenda of the struggle for liberation. African-American churches, schools, and social and political organizations have been the traditional institutions of moral development, and they would continue to be so in this process. I know no better way to battle the DCPC than by getting the proactive involvement of the community itself in the establishment of spiritual and moral values. Racism is too large a target for an effective and focused movement with the potential to reach a clearly defined objective. Furthermore, racism is not the sole enemy. The DCPC is profoundly dangerous because it destroys one's spiritual foundation. Stopping the DCPC is a fight that can be won. The fight must now focus on self-development. Racism has devastated the African-American spirit and harmed the social reality of African Americans. However, youths with the DCPC regard their destructive behavior as their only alternative. The principles in this book will foster a deep sense of community and responsibility. The statistics released by the U.S. Department of Justice, the National Urban League, and the NAACP suggest that the state of African Americans youths worsened in the 1990s. They indicate that African Americans make up less than

13 percent of the U.S. population, but about 48 percent of the prison population. There were 288,133 African-Americans arrested for violent crimes in 1994, and 10,420 were arrested for murders. A total of 62,628 of these crimes were committed by youths under the age of 18. The unemployment rate for African-American youths at risk remained high even during the booming economy of the late 1990s. According to the U.S. Department of Labor, the unemployment rate of African Americans between the ages of 16 and 19 was 23% in 1998. The unemployment rate of those between the ages of 20 and 24 was 17.7%.[80] The DCPC is the most destructive force confronting youths at risk. Social solutions, although helpful in its final destruction, alone will not overcome self-destruction. The lives of youths at risk will be changed only through the development of holistic spiritual awareness rooted in Black theology. The DCPC is a deadly force that will place millions more youths at risk if not dealt with swiftly, proactively, and spiritually. The fight for liberation must focus on youths, particularly those at risk. The youths of the 1950s, 1960s, and 1970s who went to jail for civil rights act were not at risk. It is significant that the youths during the periods mentioned above were the ones who led the African-American community in several important movements. Martin Luther King, Jr. was only 25 when he led the Montgomery Bus Boycott. Malcolm X was only 27 when he joined the Nation of Islam. Those who are at risk today must become the leaders in the struggle for community liberation because they possess the energy, but it is presently misguided. They are right now on the wrong side, and must be won to the side of the community.

These ten principles were identified to aid African-American youths at risk understand that materialism and racism led to their self-destructiveness. The problems are the DCPC and nihilism. The solution is to teach youths at risk to acquire spiritual awareness that will change their destructive behavior patterns, help them find meaning, and successfully assimilate into a highly challenging and technological economy. These spiritual values are rooted in Black theology. This will be new territory for Black theology in its emphasis on proactive spiritual education. This self-destructive behavior is a learned behavior that is acquired in a nihilistic culture. Youths with the DCPC pass it on to others through peer pressure, friendship bonds, and gang identification necessary for survival in nihilistic neighborhoods.

The establishment of a spiritual morality to nurture the most vulnerable in the African-American community will be a major step toward defeating the DCPC and winning the war against self-destruction. The real objective is to defeat the DCPC by teaching African-Americans how to change self-destructive behavior patterns. The DCPC has become a destructive force that, like racism, oppresses in profound ways. Slavery was very oppressive, but it never destroyed the spirituality of the slaves. History has taught us that slavery is not the worst thing that can happen to a people because a spiritually centered and determined people will overcome it.

However, when a people destroys its own spiritual compass, it also destroys its hope. The elimination of racism is not the sole solution. It is not a realistic goal. My vision is for the African-American community to become so self-reliant, financially wise, and spiritually focused that racism will no longer be an insurmountable obstacle to social progress and spiritual stability in the African-American experience. My strategy seeks to make racism less devastating by emphasizing self-reliance and spiritual stability as keys to financial stability. The goal is to give youths at risk the skills and tools for meaningful and empowered living. These ten spiritual principles will help vulnerable youths at risk gain inner healing, emotional maturity, a sense of community, cultural pride, economic potential, political awareness, and genuine education. Furthermore, they will cultivate a spiritual morality that will make them identify with the struggle for community liberation. This morality will deter them from living by the nihilism of the Destructive Capitalistic Personality Complex.

# 7

# The Ten Principles of Spiritual Healing

This final chapter challenges the African-American community by offering a simple solution to the problem of nihilism and the DCPC. The conclusions that I make in no way blame the African-American community for widespread nihilism nor do they place blame solely on racism. I do not advocate the views of traditional liberalism or traditional conservatism, but put together principles from a Black theology that grew out of years of oppression. These are the spiritual principles that are absent from the lives, activities, and experiences of many young African-Africans. These spiritual principles of Black theology are crucial for today's troubled youths because they are at risk of acquiring the DCPC and leading lives of immorality and crime. The DCPC leads them to live a life motivated by selfish economic gain. Their lives reflect their total lack of interest in the liberation of the African-American community. It is because of a lack of leadership development and the rise of immoral leadership that no goals for liberation that appealed to the masses were established. Furthermore, a process for human spiritual and moral development structured in the institutions of the African-American community ended when segregation ended as a principle. The demise of this process has hindered the rise of a movement. There are really no substantive liberation goals that are drawing the masses into a movement and there is no liberation movement operating in the African-American community. The Million Man March was the closest thing to a movement of this nature in recent years. There are individual churches and mosques taking the leadership role in this area in a small segment of the African-American community. The entire fabric of the African-American community has changed in the past 25 to 30 years. These spiritual principles have been developed from the Black theology of theologians and ministers such as Martin Luther King, Jr., Malcolm X, James Cone, Deotis Roberts, Noel Erskine, Ralph Abernathy, Joseph L. Roberts, Jr., Charles G. Adams, and Wyatt Tee Walker. The ultimate goal is to bring the community together through the church to establish self-reliance as a means to liberation. The principle of self-reliance is both positive and proactive; it is not a reactive response to racism and does not operate from the notion that

African Americans' present circumstances are due solely to racism. The principle of self-reliance does not fail to recognize the impact of racism, but takes the position that real personal and communal power will be realized when African-Americans are proactive and do not think of themselves solely as victims. The victim mentality directs all of its energy toward alleviating racism, but fighting racism is a war African Americans cannot win. Furthermore, only those who are racist have the power to change their racism, whereas African Americans need to utilize their energy on focusing on self-reliance. Additionally, self-reliance gives African Americans control over their goals of liberation because they would depend upon only their own will and energy. In the twenty-first century we must take our spiritual, social, and economic destinies in our own hands with self-reliance as the means.

## Spiritual Values and the African-American Experience

The work of Ronald Mincy, the editor of the book, *Nurturing Young Black Males*, is both interesting and important in the discussion of changing the destructive behavior patterns of youths at risk. Like my approach, his is Afrocentric. Mincy uses a universal approach that he believes is applicable to African cultures around the world, whereas my approach is based solely on the African-American experiences in the U.S. from slavery to the present. The spiritual principles identified here are applicable only in the African-American context. I have identified spiritual principles that very likely were established by the institutions of the African-American community before integration, and were transmitted to individuals by way of the family, school, church, and oral tradition. The principles I have identified emerged from the Black theology spiritual traditions and experiences in slavery and developed within the African-American community in its struggle for respect and justice. These spiritual principles bring spiritual meaning and communal awareness, and together they will promote a sense of self-pride, personal power, and community identity. Ultimately this community identity will change the attitude that is responsible for perpetuating destructive behavior patterns. These behavior patterns will change when attitudes change. The church and the mosque are the institutions that remain in the community with the spiritual muscle and influence that have the capacity to cultivate these spiritual principles in at risk youths. The essential principles are grounded in a spiritual tradition that has been revered, taught to African-Americans, then related to the overall struggle for justice. The problem of the DCPC is spiritual, and the only meaningful solution for healing is spiritual. The proposed values are spiritual substance that will change attitudes such as the DCPC and ultimately foster moral behavior. Mincy's assessments are insightful, but the present approach and context are quite different. Community influence is of equal importance as that of the family. In fact, in the African-American experience in the U.S., the community influenced the development of family values. Since African Americans were emancipated from slavery, the church has been the engine of the process that developed spiritual principles, which are responsible for cultivating family and community values. The African-American family is a by-product of the community. These essential principles spring from African-American spirituality.

According to Mincy, these African family values are ethical principles that guide the conduct of African family members, and he refers to these values as the "Seven Rs." He identifies the first four ethical principles as the work of anthropologist Niara Sudarkasa; they are respect, responsibility, reciprocity, and restraint. He adds three more: religion, rhythm, and redemption. According to Mincy, Sudarkasa asserts that respect is the core principle because it governs proper behavior both within the family and society at large. Responsibility is the acceptance of an obligation established by one's self to create and maintain a productive and united family life, and this behavior is rewarded in kind by other members of the family. Reciprocity is key because it establishes the ongoing process of continued good deeds within the family structure. Restraint simply means that the rights of a family member are balanced by the needs of the group. For Mincy, religion in African societies is not written on paper but is in the hearts, minds, oral history, and ritual. He maintains that belief and action are inseparable in the African tradition. Rhythm is important to the self-image of Africans. It flows in customs, work, play, war, sex, speech, worship, song, and dance. Redemption emerges from the worldview that life never dies.[81] Mincy brings passion and scholarship to the suggestions he makes for the nurturing needs of young black males.

It is important to understand that in the African-American experience family values and community values are one and the same. They are the values grounded in African-American spiritual traditions and embraced by the community in the struggle for liberation, an effort to find hope in the midst of dehumanization. Family and community values are the same in the sense that they are grounded and shaped in the African-American religious and spiritual experiences and are means to establish human dignity. Spiritual awareness and faith in a just God who is both healer and liberator gave substance, hope, direction, and meaning in the fight against oppression in the African-American experience. This was the case with Harriet Tubman's Underground Railroad, Martin L. King, Jr.'s, dream, Malcolm X's vision of self-reliance, and the teachings of visionaries such as Sojourner Truth, Bishop Richard Allen, Bishop Henry McNeal Turner, and Elijah Muhammad.

## Spiritual Awareness: An Attitude in the Fight for Liberation

Some of the values referred to here are conveyed in the song "We Shall Overcome." When it was sung during the Civil Rights Movement it symbolized a people possessed with a faith to trust God for liberation. "We Shall Overcome" expresses an attitude of spiritual awareness, self-love, community unity, hope, discipline, and determination, all to be put into action for the common good of the entire community. It was an attitude that captured the true meaning of what it meant to sacrifice and fight in order to gain liberation. With this attitude were those important spiritual values that were taught and preached in the African-American spiritual experience. The "We Shall Overcome" attitude was informed by values that brought a sense of personal pride and community dignity. It is essential to understand that family and community values are both grounded in the African-American spiritual experiences. This realization is indispensable to a discussion of Black theology, the African-American church/mosque, and the key spiritual principles that have nurtured and empowered millions of African-Americans to reach their highest human potential. Spiritual awareness is the key to understanding this traditional value system that has been in the African-American experience for the past 500 years, but has been replaced with the DCPC that has overcome thousands of youths at risk in recent decades.

## Spiritual Awareness and the DCPC

The Destructive Capitalistic Personality Complex (DCPC) has left thousands of African-American youths spiritually and morally challenged and at risk of crime, drug abuse, and other destructive behavioral patterns. The first step in the process of healing is to teach youths at risk the first principle, spiritual awareness. Spiritual awareness provides the substance that can change one's worldview, understanding of self and community, and moral code with which one governs one's life. In other words, internal change will produce external results. Destructive behavior patterns are the external manifestations of internal spiritual, moral, and social conflict and a struggle for personal meaning. This internal conflict generates confusion, anger, a cold-hearted disregard for human life, a lack of respect for traditional African-American spiritual values, insecurity and low self-esteem, disregard for the African-American community's cause, and a self-centered desire for material gain by any means necessary. The only hope for internal conflict of this nature is spiritual awareness, which is the first essential step toward self-liberation, which includes spiritual identity, moral discipline, personal power and purpose, and community belonging. Spiritual awareness in this sense is the substance that will open the eyes of youths at risk and change the destructive behavior patterns of an entire generation. Spiritual awareness is the first step toward healing for those who have lost their way from the spiritual tradition that served as a source of strength and a mechanism of survival for African Americans. It has the power to break new spiritual ground within the soul and form a new moral foundation within the personality.

The DCPC and spiritual awareness cannot be present in one's character simultaneously; each develops an attitude for living that dictates opposing behavioral patterns. You either live under the destructive attitude of the DCPC or the enlightenment and morality of spiritual awareness. The DCPC is the reason that too many youths live by the ethos "I just want to get paid". They will steal, kill, or do whatever it takes to get a piece of the wealth in the U.S. They lack respect for human life and the common good of their community.

Gaining a deep spiritual awareness is the turning point that will reverse the DCPC, and will positively affect the way at risk youths interpret their environment. Most importantly, spiritual awareness will function as a principle and inner-guide for making moral choices. For example, prior to his imprisonment Malcolm X had the DCPC; it was not called the DCPC, but he possessed all the symptoms of the DCPC during those years. However, he experienced what I call a transformational crisis. This transformational crisis led to the development of his spiritual awareness while in prison, and this spiritual experience changed the way he understood the world as well as the life he chose. Spiritual awareness is the inner substance necessary for developing a moral foundation that will reverse destructive behavior patterns caused by the DCPC, and a transformational crisis is the experience that will make spiritual awareness the living principle in one's life. The choice of spiritual awareness is a choice made by each individual. The philosopher and theologian Immanuel

Kant (1724–1804) believed that all human beings are born with a spiritual nature. The individual will make the right choice when he or she attains the cognitive insights and the social reinforcement to do so, which will come from individuals or institutions. In the case of Malcolm X, his newly discovered spiritual awareness initiated his self-liberating process, which began with self-examination, which led to self-dissatisfaction, which led to self-evaluation, which finally led to self-realization. His spiritual awareness put him in touch with a spiritual aspect of himself that he did not know before, and a crisis was the experience that transformed him completely. Spiritual awareness leads to self-enlightenment, purpose, social awareness, and community identity. A transformational crisis is the experience that will cause youths to lose the DCPC, and its destructive behavioral patterns. However, youths at risk have an innate spiritual nature, which gives them the ability to learn spiritual principles. When they are guided by individuals and institutions they have come to trust and respect, and who they believe are concerned for their well-being, spiritual awareness will become a reality.

Spiritual awareness is the means to developing personal power. Personal power is achieved when one acquires faith in God and in one's self to realize dreams that appear to be impossible because of poverty and lack of opportunity. Personal power gave me the tools to understand racism and provided inner resources for survival. It helped me develop practical wisdom. I learned this wisdom from mentors and the oral tradition of my community. I was empowered with the wisdom to deal with racism and to stay focused on personal and community goals. Furthermore, I gained wisdom that enabled me to envision a better society in the midst of the ugliness of dehumanization. I developed an inner joy and peace that made me face personal setbacks with fortitude, and the energy to set and plan realistic goals. One of the essential values I learned from mentors and the wise oral tradition in my community and in the African-American community as a whole was to treat racism as a temporary setback rather than as a permanent problem.

## Self-Reliance is the Goal—The Demise of Racism is Not

When African Americans are passive and reactive and blame racism for much of their despair, they have let racism pre-empt them of their personal power rather than utilizing that power to change their conditions. The preoccupation with the effects of racism often becomes an obstacle to what should be their goal, to pool community resources so that there is the power to make better choices. We have power over our choices, and we need to make substantive choices that will improve our personal lives and our community. Additionally, we give racism complete power and control over our destiny when we wage a war solely against it. As previously mentioned, this is a war that cannot be won because there is no weapon that can redeem a racist heart. Historically this redemption has been difficult to accomplish. There are racists who avow Christianity as their faith. In many cases religious institutions have failed to change a racist heart into a loving one. In their reactive actions and preoccupation with the power that racism has African Americans put themselves in the position of dependence upon others for their justice. Consequently, their oppressors began to view them as persons without the personal power to succeed, persons who want a handout and preferential treatment. The power to achieve liberation was given to powers outside of the African-American community. The story of African-Americans is a spiritual one much like that of the people of Moses as written in the Holy Hebrew text of Exodus, and the God of African-Americans is the same as the God of the Holy Bible, who is the God of the oppressed. It is time to focus on self-reliance and utilize spiritual, personal, and community powers on that which African Americans have the power to change. Malcolm X envisioned a community that would take its destiny in its own hands, and this is the type of community that I believe is the solution to nihilism. The powers outside of the African-American community will never be a better friend to it than the community will be to itself. Black theology in all of its forms and traditions teaches that God, and the faith, spiritual strength, and determination of an oppressed people are the elements that make up the powerful combination that can defeat oppression.

## The Development of Afrocentrism and the Deconstruction of Individualism

The notion that African Americans will rise or have risen solely by their own bootstraps is a false myth. It is more realistic to acknowledge the historical reality of the African American experience, that African Americans have found liberation when they have united to struggle together with God at the center. The success of Justice Clarence Thomas was not due solely to his own merits, nor was it due solely to the help of his political allies. It was what he learned in his community that empowered him to walk through Yale University, head the U.S. Equal Employment Opportunity Office, and sit on the U.S. Supreme Court. Individual success without support from the community is possible, but not likely within the African-American experience. Afrocentrism is the worldview that is informed by African cultural contributions and that promotes a community approach to individual and community development. It functions as a collective approach to attaining liberation.

Prior to integration most African-American communities functioned with the interest and the common good of all members in the community. The community embraced fundamental principles to obtain individual, family, and community development and liberation. This collective community effort for the interest of all is a basic element of Afrocentrism. This interdependence among individuals, families, churches, and schools to achieve justice began on the slave plantation and continued; the influence that African-American institutions had upon interdependent families and the larger community was a primary element of Afrocentrism in the US. In an Afrocentric community, there are many persons who contribute to an individual's personality formation, and are most proud when that person succeeds; they see it as a community achievement.

It must be noted that historically individualism, which is at the core of Western thought, does not work and will never work to bring healing and liberation to the African-American community. For example, we are living during one of the most prosperous periods in U.S. history, and some African Americans have benefited, but if one were to look at the African-American community in its entirety, one would never know that the U.S. is experiencing such great prosperity. The DCPC is being acquired by an entire generation because they are insecure and believe that in order to gain their part of the American dream, they must acquire wealth through immoral means. Individualism inspires individuals to focus on acquiring wealth for self in order to obtain economic and social well-being. African Americans have adopted individualism, and this mindset has become so widespread in the African-American community that it has caused the destruction of structures that provided moral leadership to the African-American community. Nihilism and the DCPC are the results.

It is significant that it was individual self-interest rather than community interest that resulted in a large number of African Americans leaving the African-American community. The theme song of the Civil Rights Movement of the 1960s and 1970s, "We Shall Overcome", captured it best. This song conveys a powerful spiritual meaning that made it difficult for most African Americans not to become indelibly influenced by its message to share in the vision of making freedom a reality for all African Americans. Spiritual awareness is the key principle that can save youths at risk from the powerful grip of the DCPC. Afrocentrism is the community approach. It is significant that the African proverb, "It takes a village to raise a child" and the song, "We Shall Overcome" believe the community and the family to be interdependent. The above mentioned proverb and song capture the meaning of community in the African-American experience; they demonstrate that family and community values are the same. They are the same in the sense that they are formed by a family and a community grounded in a deep sense of spiritual oneness and interdependence and that need to obtain freedom. Spiritual awareness is the means to move from individualism to Afrocentrism and from self-interest to community interest.

## Spiritual and Moral Development

### Integration and the Disappearance of Community Institutions

Before further discussion of the values and the institutions that reinforced them, it is important to point out that with integration came the dismantlement of these structures of human development and community strength. Integration needed to take place at some point in order to bring wholeness to U.S. society, but in retrospect the African-American community may have been too vulnerable for such an immediate and drastic social transition. The timing of integration is a significant element for consideration in the attempt to make a fair assessment of the deleterious developments within the African-American community since integration. To be uprooted from one's school and to lose mentors and nurturing neighbors were immeasurable losses in one's process of human growth and development. It was akin to losing a parent and growing up without that love and support. African-American leaders were thoroughly focused on the issue of African Americans enjoying civil rights. Therefore, they invested their energies on bringing about integration; they were optimistic that integration was the answer to the issue of equality. Overall integration was good for U.S. society. However, since freedom from slavery was a relatively recent event, the survival of key institutions were at risk because many were still in the developmental stages and were not established enough to survive. In-depth study into the response of humans when confronted with the loss of social symbols, whether they are institutions, individuals, or traditions would have revealed that chaotic behavior is often the result. Cultural anthropologist Clifford Geertz clarified the meaning of cultural symbols in human behavior. Geertz's book, *Interpretation of Cultures*, published in 1973, discusses changes in human behavior after the loss of symbols.[82] In addition, Geertz uses two other important works to conduct his study of the affects of cultural symbols upon human behavior. The works are: K. Burke's, *The Philosophy of Literary Form: Studies in Symbolic Action* and S. Langer's, *Philosophy in a New Key*.[83] These works were available and should have been used to conduct a serious study on changes in human behavior when confronted with the loss of symbols within the context of the African-American community. Elijah Muhammad's Black Muslim Organization did create new symbols in the African-American community. These key institutions established themselves as support structures for the process of human development, but they were not stable enough to survive integration. Furthermore, the demise of the support structures provided by churches, schools, families, and mentors adversely affected spiritual development. A systematic and more gradual move toward integration would have saved African-American spiritual, social, educational, and economic structures.

In his essay, "Moral Development for African-American Leadership," Peter J. Paris reaches the same conclusion on how the elimination of segregation as a principle has adversely affected the ability of black families, schools, and churches to promote human development. Paris maintains that key institutions in the African-American community were responsible for moral development. He believes that black families, schools, and churches shared a common moral ethos. He argues that parents, teachers, and clergy functioned as moral examples because they embodied the community's basic values, and by precept and example, transmitted them effectively from one generation to the next. It was due mainly to the collaborative efforts of black families, schools, and churches, in the midst of a hostile white world, that a black world of moral integrity was created and maintained and served as the uniting force for progress and liberation. Paris's conclusion is right on the mark when he says that the destruction of racial segregation as a principle of dehumanization greatly threatened the principle of humanization that emerged within segregation. Further, this social vulnerability has had a vital role in promoting a negative self-image in many African-American youths and the present unhealthy social environment. This social breakdown ushered in the nihilism that has resulted in the formation of the DCPC. Nihilism is a serious problem for the African-American community as a whole. However, nihilism is no excuse, and does not account for the 597,000 African-Americans in prison, of which 558,700 are males, and the 221,000 other African-American inmates in local city jails across the nation, according to 1999 U.S. Department of Justice statistics.[84]

My point is that there are no longer support structures for moral development. Consequently, many youths at risk lose hope and give up because of negative, unsupportive experiences in schools, and as a result many may never develop the desire to pursue education as a means to their goals. The alternative is the streets, where they will likely develop the DCPC. Serious social consequences have been the result, many of them the effect of the desegregation of public schools, which brought about the loss of the black moral ethos within the public schools. African-American students for several decades have experienced public schools as unfriendly, alien spaces uninterested in their well-being. According to Paris, public schools are experienced as out of sync with the values of African-American families, churches, and the larger African-American community.[85]

## The Moral Value of Education

Before integration, the same structures that were present in most African-American communities and provided the principles for moral development were present in my small town of Thomasville, Georgia. My community gave me seven important values that were reinforced by four institutions. These spiritual and moral values provided me with practical skills that improved my development; they placed an emphasis on the principles of self-liberation, self-love, and community pride and belonging. The values are: (1) the importance of an education, (2) a strong work ethic, (3) the need to compete, (4) the African-American story, (5) family, community, and vocational responsibility, (6) reputation, respect, integrity, loyalty, commitment, and honesty, and (7) financial responsibility. The institutions that reinforced these values were: (1) the family, which established them, (2) the church, which defined, corrected, and spiritually focused them, (3) the school, which nurtured, developed, prepared, and inspired through educational development, and (4) the adult community, which cultivated wisdom through mentoring and an oral tradition.

Before I turned school age, my mother shared stories with me from a rich oral tradition that had been told to her and to her parents before her. I believe that many of these stories were created from the wisdom of a community mentor whose goal was to inspire young African Americans to pursue education as a means to liberation. Many of these stories gripped me and left an indelible impression upon my spirit. There was a story about a young African boy who worked for an old white doctor whom he assisted with patients. The young boy knew how to read so he read every medical book and journal in the doctor's office. He became a medical expert, and the entire community came to depend upon his medical expertise. The old doctor died prematurely, and many of his patients sought this young man out for medical treatment. There were many stories passed down through the oral tradition in my community, but I remember this one because I wanted to be as intelligent as this young man. To obtain an education was a matter of principle, and it was interwoven with the notion of sustaining pride in the African-American heritage and with the struggle for justice and equality. This value was promoted to inspire the community. At its root was the Black theology faith tradition. The belief in the possibility of obtaining an education was a manifestation of faith in God. Education was believed to be one of God's tools to bring liberation to His people, African Americans in an oppressive U.S. society. The ideal of obtaining an education was a principle that was deeply rooted in the African-American culture. It is significant that the issue of education became the battleground in attaining equality, with integration as the means; this issue was at the core of the Civil Rights Movement of the 1950s and 1960s. Additionally, integration was the proposed solution to educational inequity. The historic 1954 case *Brown vs. the Board of Education* was an important milestone that raised the consciousness of European-Americans and paved the way for large numbers of African Americans to get an equal education. Education was a principle that was supported and reinforced by every institution in the African-American community.

A determination to obtain an education was a personal value I developed in my segregated community in South Georgia. My parents, teachers, ministers, and many wise adults, including adults without formal education, helped etch this essential value into my psyche; it has governed my life, and I have transmitted it to others. Those people always whispered to me with love and faith that education was the key to my liberation; not even racism would be able to take it away from me. Education would guarantee me respect in my community and in society; it was my only true ticket to the freedom train. "Don't miss your train," "You must obtain an education" were messages that were consistently given to youths by families, teachers, ministers, and mentors prior to integration. James Brown's song, "Don't Be a Drop-Out" was welcomed with enthusiasm by the African-American community and quickly became a national hit in the 1960s.

Education as a necessary principle was programmed into African-Americans' psyches. It was regarded as a value that was necessary for one to become a respected and productive citizen. A negative attitude toward education was not socially acceptable; an individual with such a viewpoint would be viewed with disapproval, and parents, teachers, ministers, and mentors would instruct other youths not to befriend that person. This value was believed by the African-American community to be essential for individual and common progress and was reinforced by the institutions that were responsible for the process of moral human development. There were social consequences that would alienate one from the mainstream if one rejected this value. Education operated as an informal social filter that determined respectability within the African-American community. The community adhered to this informal social filtration, and there was competitiveness among individuals in the community who desired respect. This competitiveness spurred one to strive for educational and professional achievement under the terms of the African-American community. Individuals who rejected education as a value were alienated and viewed as counterproductive to the cause. Consequently, they were not allowed to interact meaningfully with respectable persons. These persons were socially marked, and adults instructed the youths to distance themselves from them. This alienation from the community hindered meaningful social interaction and created a social lower class based on family reputation and values. Therefore, respectable people did not date, marry, or have meaningful relationships with persons who did not value education. This was an informal social rule that was reinforced by the institutions that provided the process of moral human development. Family members, teachers, ministers, and mentors in the African-American community reinforced this social rule. They believed that it was their social and spiritual duty to prevent relationships of this nature from developing; they concluded that they hindered the community's progress. They taught that one who did not hold education as an essential value was unconcerned with future worth and would never attain it.

A well-known Baptist minister told the story of his daughter's first date. When the young man came to his house and spoke with him, he discovered that the young man did not value education. The father refused to let him date his daughter. His daughter was upset at the time because she believed that she was in love. However, he said, "today my daughter is a medical doctor and her husband is as well; she now thanks me for protecting her from a relationship with a young man who is a convicted felon." The father never had to concern himself with his daughter interacting with this man outside their home because her teachers and others reinforced his wishes at school and in the community.

There is a myth from the oral tradition that suggests that involvement with the socially unacceptable will ultimately lead to becoming one of them. This was also a famous saying in the African-American community. Education was regarded by the African-American community as an essential value necessary to establish personal worth and common progress.

In his book, *The Mis-Education of the Negro*, Carter Woodson points out that educated African Americans often remained unemployed in spite of their education. Woodson understood that African-American unemployment is in some cases the result of discrimination. The educational system was biased against Africa. It taught African Americans a negative self-image, and did not aim to provide them with an authentic education. The education that African-Americans received was inadequate; quite often they did not obtain the training and the skills necessary for meaningful employment. His conclusions were reached by utilizing a sociological analysis and unemployment findings on the U.S. economy in the 1930s; his work offered tremendous insight to leaders during the civil rights movements of the 1950s, 1960s, and 1970s, who used them and focused on passing legislation making discrimination illegal. There is hope for the educated and skilled unemployed African-American, but there is less so for the individual unemployed because of lack of education and training. The uneducated unemployed and underemployed are more likely to turn to crime and self-destruction as their solution to oppression, but the educated will more likely thrive because of their empowerment. In the African-American experience, education as a spiritual principle functioned as a means to improve the community by first improving the individual. It improves the individual's vocational potential and humanistic knowledge. It broadens one's worldview and ability to understand and critique one's social conditions.

Education provides the skills for one to make oneself and community better. However, personal power provides the spiritual substance to fight for what one has come to believe. Personal power transcends the conditions of oppression. For example, Harriet Tubman had personal power in spite of not having much formal education, as did many other slaves. With her personal power she was able to lead one of the most successful liberation efforts, the Underground Railroad. However, it is more practical to have both. Personal power is spiritual power to overcome external oppressive conditions. Education provides the necessary skills to critique oppressive systems and formulate effective solutions. This is an essential and practical quality of education in the process of developing personal power. Education played a key role in Rosa Parks' courageous decision to refuse to give up her bus seat. It gave Martin L. King, Jr., the insight to spearhead the Poor People's Campaign in spite of the fact that there were threats on his life, and it gave Malcolm X the wisdom to promote self-pride. It is essential for youths at risk to gain the spiritual substance that is within the traditional African-American perspective on education. It will provide them with personal power. By taking education as a value they will have taken one more step toward self-liberation. They need this value to understand their story and to gain the personal power necessary not to fall victim to the DCPC.

## Responsibility

Responsibility has been a meaningful principle, grounded in spirituality, in guiding conduct within the African-American community. There are three distinct primary types of responsibility that are spiritual values in the African-American experience. They are community responsibility, family responsibility, and vocational responsibility. Needless to say there are also other types of responsibility that are important spiritual values in the African-American experience.

### Community Responsibility

Community responsibility in the African-American experience grew out of oppression in slavery. As previously mentioned, family values and community values are virtually the same. The nature of African-American oppression caused severe family brokenness. During slavery family members were separated, and from this despair a fundamental interdependence developed among African-American slaves as a means of survival. This interdependence continued among post-slavery African Americans, and there was a strong sense of responsibility toward each other. The African-American community became a large interdependent village with an informal network that had a powerful influence in human development. This informal network established standards and rules to guide conduct within the African-American community in order to cultivate individuals who would be good for the community. Additionally, the most educated, the professionally accomplished, the elderly, and church leaders were the persons active in the informal network, whose primary function was to advance the community's interest. These leaders determined the goals, function, and focus of the community in its struggle for justice. The churches and schools were the focus of community pride and accomplishment, but the church was the primary institution for social change and progress, particularly since the church was responsible for establishing many schools and colleges. The influence of the church reached every institution in the African-American community, including the family, civil rights organizations, businesses, and schools; it continued the interdependence that was established during slavery. This bond among African Americans was spiritual in nature and generated a deep sense of community identity, loyalty, unity, and responsibility. The sense of closeness shared in this community bond was stimulated and intensified for two practical reasons: (1) the bond emerged in the midst of suffering with a strong faith that provided them with wisdom, patience, and strategies to find liberation; (2) these were common experiences they all shared, identified with, and understood. Family brokenness had a powerful impact upon the African-American community. It made the community vulnerable to even more oppression and created an urgent need for leadership. It engendered compassion and a sense of responsibility toward each other, and inspired individuals to assume leadership responsibility out of love for their community; it cultivated an urgent desire for freedom and equality, and made people receptive to spirituality and a faith with a message of hope. These factors in the African-American experience played an important role in the development of this informal network and the process of human moral development. Responsibility as a value made the formation of the network possible. The power at the core of the informal network that made it possible to operate was spiritual in nature. This faith has its roots in the Black theology faith traditions that started on the slave plantations and were later used as a meaningful tool for human development and for the fight for liberation. The origin of the sense of responsibility and the power of the network was community despair. Both responsibility and the network had a spiritual dynamic at their core that served to bring liberation to the community. The community played a major role in reconnecting a disconnected family structure and cultivating a process of moral and spiritual human development.

### Family Responsibility

Family responsibility encompasses another principle within the family structure, reputation. A family's reputation is the reflection of its integrity. It is the product of the way the collective conduct of a family is perceived by the community. When family members are known to be honorable, the community will have a positive perception of that family's conduct and a positive reputation will be established.

The family is the most important institution in the African-American community, and the community has historically had a powerful impact upon family formation, the development of its value system, and its level of participation within the community. The goal of the informal network responsible for the process of spiritual and moral human development was to form strong families through responsible adults. This was an obligation the community adopted. The African-American family is built on the same premise. Family members share the responsibility to devote their talents, time, and energy to the common welfare of the family. Family members guided their conduct by this ethos. Family members, like the informal network within the African-American community, made commitments to forego self-interest for the common good of the family and the development of family members. The common welfare of the family was first and foremost, and everyone within the family shared this vision. For example, it was common to make financial or housekeeping contributions for the upkeep and function of family life. Disagreements about the quantity and quality of people's contributions occurred, but did not change the nature of this common responsibility within the family structure.

In the African-American community, family reputation was determined by the community's perception of the family's conduct. A family's reputation became bad when the community perceived that its conduct did not adhere to its spiritual and moral standards and to its struggle for justice and equality. A main role of the informal network was to provide leadership development for the interest of the community. The self-interest of the community helped the community to emerge as a powerful influence upon family life in general. The community's influence upon families and the behavior of its members was a reality established by the informal network. The responsibility of protecting the family's reputation was a responsibility that was taken seriously by family members, and the informal network influenced families' moral and spiritual values; these values were products of community self-interest, but they also influenced the formation of the African-American family. For example, older siblings took a direct interest in the behaviors and activities of younger siblings; they did so out of a sense of responsibility to them and concern for the family's reputation. They hoped to prevent teenagers from engaging in sexual, criminal, and dishonorable activities. Furthermore, younger teenage daughters were not allowed to attend school dances and other activities without being accompanied by an older brother, sister, or other relative. A family decision to allow a daughter to date too soon could jeopardize its reputation. When the informal network thought that it was too soon, some families would put an end to it.

Community perception of family conduct had a direct connection with the self-image and pride that the community gained; positive self-image and pride inspired the work toward development and were projected to larger U.S. society. Therefore, spiritual and moral principles, community pride, and the cause of justice and equality were transmitted to the family through responsibility as a precept; the family transmitted these values to family members. Family responsibility is an obligation to cultivate honor, which will enhance the family's reputation within the community, which was believed to serve the common good of the community. Honorable behavior was believed to serve the community's goals.

## Vocational Responsibility

It is important to discuss the origins of the work ethic as a moral value, which was established through family reputation. The informal network influenced the development of the work ethic in the African-American family. If the informal network's perception of a father's work ethic were poor, his family members would tend to be perceived as having a poor work ethic as well. However, in such instances, other family members still had the opportunity to develop a reputation of their own. Mentors and other responsible persons in the community took the responsibility of teaching those without family role models a good work ethic. This arose out of community self-interest. It was an essential aspect of the process of leadership development in the African-American community that was provided by the informal network.

The foundation for work as a moral value was established in the shared responsibilities required of members in family life. As previously mentioned, family responsibility included work contributions to the upkeep of family life.

Performing assigned tasks at home exhibited loyalty and commitment to the daily productivity of family life. Additionally, families utilized this as a means to teach the work ethic as a moral value and to establish the 200 percent work principle within family members. African Americans transmitted this 200 percent principle through an oral tradition based on experiences in the work world. European-American work superiors judged the work of African-Americans through the lens of racism, which required African Americans to perform superior work in order to be viewed as satisfactory employees. The wisdom behind this 200 percent principle was twofold. In the family it was believed that if one gave 200 percent it was returned by the family and in life.

In the work world, it was believed that if one gave 200 percent in work performance, the reward was job stability. However, work evaluations were based on the perceptions of work superiors. The reality of discrimination in the workplace gave life and credibility to the 200 percent principle. Therefore, it was essential that family and community leaders taught the value of work in a way in which it would be grasped, adopted, and applied in one's life. A good work ethic enhanced one's reputation. The spiritual inspiration behind the work ethic was simple: God bestowed one with blessings and opportunities for one's commitment and loyalty to one's family, community, and self. Family leaders were responsible for teaching other members the importance of performing work with pride and responsibility to self, family, and community. Work as a moral value served as a tool to cultivate a strong work ethic, which would prepare people for job security and furthering the cause of equality and justice.

## Self-Reliance: A Contemporary Challenge

As previously mentioned, widespread nihilism is the primary cause of the fundamental breakdown in the spiritual and moral self of youths at risk. The DCPC is the end product, which is largely due to personality formation taking place in the midst of a nihilistic environment. I pointed out that the structure for human spiritual and moral development that had been in place within the African-American community since slavery is no longer present. The absence of such a significant structure leaves youths without meaningful spiritual and moral leadership and at risk of acquiring the DCPC. This process of human spiritual and moral development influenced the family and community values within the African-American community prior to the elimination of segregation as a principle. Today the challenge for the African-American community is to replace this structure for spiritual and moral development that disappeared in the 1970s with a new structure.

The Christian church and the Muslim mosque need to take the lead since they are the most influential institutions with the resources to establish a structure of this nature. These conclusions do not ignore racism's contributions to much of African-American despair, but racism is an infinite attitude that is part of the personality of a large number of Americans. Racism is an attitude that is fostered by cultural symbols, traditional values, community demographics, political ideologies, and social structures. Racism is established in businesses and religion. The burden of fighting racism does not belong solely to African Americans or other people of color. The struggle against racism is one that all Americans must share and requires the efforts of all persons of integrity and faith. There is nothing that African Americans can do about the problem of racism that religion, faith, and the teachings of Jesus have not done. To focus efforts against racism will be a misuse of collective energy and resources, besides being illogical. I do not deny that there were social policies that contributed to the despair and nihilism that are so prevalent in the African-American community. African Americans must have a strong voice against policies detrimental to their interests and remain activist in the political process. However, the African-American community must go beyond being reactive and be proactive, moving toward self-reliance. We must resolve to make better choices, and teach our youths to do so as they plan for the future.

The Catholic Church found itself at odds with the public educational system in the U.S. The Catholic Church believed that it was important to have faith integrated into the education curriculum for the overall development of Catholic students. Catholic schools were the result. The solution to the dilemma of nihilism in the African-American community is complex. A plan of action toward a solution includes that African Americans focus on the development of a spiritual and moral structure to prevent the spread of nihilism, establish a process for the moral and spiritual development of youths at risk, and create a more self-reliant African-American community. The more than 400 billion dollars earned each year by African Americans must be used for their own spiritual, political, and economic advantage. The focus must be on self-reliance. It must be etched into the souls of African Americans to inspire them to assume the responsibility for self, family, and community which I have described in this chapter. The first step in this liberation process will be to focus primarily on the development of a spiritual and moral structure that will stop the spread of nihilism. Significant aspects of Malcolm X's ideas on self-reliance merit a reevaluation. In order to establish a new process of human spiritual and moral development, a break from the values and influences of western individualism, which has become more prevalent in the thought and actions of African Americans, is the first necessary step. A reconnection to Afrocentric values and the community mechanisms established in slavery, which remained in the community until segregation ended as a principle, is the second step. The challenge of promoting self-reliance will be to develop in the African-American community a similar structure for the process of human spiritual and moral development. A process of this nature in the midst of a nihilistic environment can bring healing to youths at risk and lead to the elimination of the DCPC.

## A Historical Perspective on African-American Behavioral Patterns and Financial Responsibility

In his book, *Black Lies, White Lies, the Truth According to Tony Brown*, Tony Brown tells the story of an African-American entrepreneur named Rick Singletary whose business failed because of a lack of African-American support. Singletary opened the largest African-American-owned and operated grocery market in the country in Columbus, Ohio. He spent his life savings, funds from his mother, and a small government-insured loan, spending 4.4 million dollars. The size of the business project provided a rare opportunity to improve this community and was hoped to be a step toward self-reliance. He opened this business in the heart of the African-American community. His vision was to create meaningful jobs that would provide benefits to African Americans, and he hoped that his business would establish a sense of community pride and accomplishment. A feasibility study concluded that there was a need for this type of supermarket as well as a customer base to support its size. Furthermore, the study found that the African Americans in the community spent 2.5 million dollars per week on groceries. He needed only a $200,000-a-week volume to keep his 130 African-American employees working. He needed less than 10 percent of the amount of money that African Americans spent each week for groceries, but his business failed and he went bankrupt. What were the behavior patterns of the people of that community, and what caused them to ignore or reject this self-help effort? How could this supermarket not succeed when it required less than 10 percent of the total that African Americans spent for groceries?

Weeks prior to the failure of this supermarket, an educational process called the "Buy Freedom Campaign of Black Economic Empowerment" was organized and supported by Tony Brown and others in an effort to prevent this business from failing. However, it was too late and the supermarket still had to close.[86] This educational process was such an essential component to raising the consciousness of the people in the community that it should have been initiated before the store opened. Educational processes are of primary importance to the development of self-reliance in the African-American community. The behavior exhibited by the African Americans who did not support the supermarket was self-destructive.

Historically, the economic behavioral patterns of African Americans have worked against self-reliance. It has roots in African-American experiences of oppression. The tendency of African Americans to work against their collective interest is discussed in Carter G. Woodson's book, *The Mis-Education of the Negro. H*is discussion of self-love and self-discipline are detailed as well.[87] There is a direct connection between African-Americans' lack of self-discipline in acting in their interest and their lack of self-love, and this entire psychological dilemma is related to having received an education that taught African Americans a negative sense of self. Furthermore, the social structure established on slave plantations spawned the perceived superiority of a light skin tone and the need of validation from slave owners.

The psychological phenomenon that causes the tendency of African Americans to act against their self-interest has roots in slavery. On slave plantations there was a social structure that rewarded light skin and penalized dark skin. People adapt their behavior to increase their chances of survival within their environment. This was the case with the slaves. In this demeaning social context where light skin was rewarded and validated, it was likely for a dark-skinned slave to desire light skin because it was associated with better treatment. This false perception of light skin as being better than dark skin distorted the slaves' sense of self and created an inferiority complex. Slaves developed a need to receive validation from the slave owner, which meant better treatment and social status on the plantation. Slaves aspired to become favored servants of the slave owner. E. Franklin Frazier in his book, *Black Bourgeoisie: The Rise of a New Middle Class*, describes the social life of slaves as being tension-filled. There was a social distinction between the house servants, who enjoyed better treatment and prestige, and the field servants, who experienced worse treatment and lower status. Many house servants had European-American ancestors. Their mixed race was more highly valued by both slaves and slave owners. These slaves held the European part of their ethnic heritage in higher esteem than the African part, and valued their light skin tone and loose curly hair.[88] African-American self-doubt and need of European-Americans' validation started on slave plantations.

Subsequently, the Emancipation Proclamation that granted freedom to slaves did little to eliminate the psychological scars inflicted during slavery. As a result of their experiences in slavery, the slaves carried practical, social, and spiritual skills that served them as means of survival. These were a strong faith tradition and a collective interdependence that led to a strong sense of community. Unfortunately, they also carried the negative baggage of self-doubt that grew out of a distorted view of selfhood and skin tone, and a strong yearning to be validated by the white establishment, which now replaced the slave owners. African-American personality formation was the product of the slaves' total experiences of oppression in slavery. Consequently, the importance of skin tone was a major aspect of social interaction and human development in all aspects of life within the African-American community. This importance placed on skin tone profoundly affected all relationships, including dating, marriages, friendships, and leadership acceptance. There was a yearning for status within the African-American community, and this was manifested in behavior patterns. This preference for light skin tone directly influenced behavior patterns and established a social structure with a color bias at its center in the African-American community. It was very similar to the bias that European Americans used to oppress all African Americans. This is the complex social reality behind the unfortunate problem of African Americans' behavior patterns that act against their self-interest.[89]

Carter G. Woodson's work is a profound critique of the U.S. education system; he concluded that it was a system that taught African Americans to think negatively of Africa and African people. According to Woodson, the education system's entire approach to educating African Americans was negative at every level, from elementary school to the university. The entire educational process transmitted negative biases toward African Americans. This system severely damaged African-American self-esteem because it portrayed African history and culture as inferior. He maintained that even the teachers and missionaries who went to the South prior to the Civil War did so for social uplift and taught vocational skills rather than critical thinking. They had good intentions, but they tried to pass on their bias that European culture was superior, rather than develop self-love. Many of these teachers and missionaries were not adequately educated themselves and therefore uncritically adhered to the traditional curriculum of that time, which denigrated African culture. This education system did more psychological damage to a psyche already vulnerable and suffering from self-doubt as a result of slavery, particularly with regard to skin tone.[90]

Education is an essential step toward self-reliance. With education, the African-American community will realize its historic tendencies toward self-destructive behavior patterns. In the case of Singletary and his store, along with the feasibility study, a widespread education campaign should have been undertaken before the supermarket opened. Many African Americans supported Martin Luther King, Jr., Marcus Garvey, and Elijah Mohammad in their attempts to make a difference in their quality of life. In order to maintain optimism about the African-American community's ability to become self-reliant, past victories must be recognized and remembered. African Americans have demonstrated that they will support movements for the community's interest. However, before winning widespread support in the African-American community, these movements started an educational campaign to inform the public, an essential part of the movement itself. This was the case with King's nonviolent direct action and Garvey's economic empowerment efforts. New self-help efforts will need to organize aggressive and intensified educational campaigns; these efforts must be aggressive and intense because self-defeating behavioral patterns have existed for over 200 years. When African Americans are educated in this manner about the origin of these behavioral patterns, rather than being self-destructive by not supporting African-American-owned businesses, they may become constructive by, e.g., deliberately frequenting African-American-owned stores whenever possible.

Any attempt to develop a self-reliant African-American community without the application of these spiritual principles of self-love, self-discipline, community responsibility, and financial responsibility in the lives and behavior patterns of African Americans is impossible. The liberation of the African-American community from nihilism and the DCPC is contingent upon whether its financial resources are used to work for it and develop self-reliance. Historically, the African-American community has been vulnerable in the area of economic development, financial responsibility, and self-help; instead it focused on integration and assimilation as the means to equality. Although the pursuit of integration had good intentions, it was flawed, and the correct values about self-reliance were not espoused. I will refer to the structure of human development to explain the behavior dynamics that took place in Columbus, Ohio.

The process of human spiritual and moral development that influenced family and community values transmitted to the African-American community a negative sense of self and a need to be validated by the white establishment. I have explained the origin of this destructive belief system and how the education system perpetuated it. The fact is, the process of human development was influenced by individuals educated in this system that valued light skin tone. The tendency to seek validation from the white establishment was held by many individuals who were active in the process of human development, and they transmitted a belief system that led individuals to act against community self-interest, particularly in the area of economic empowerment. The preference for light skin tone leads people to not support African-American-owned businesses. White skin is preferred to any African-American skin tone when this destructive psychological dynamic is at work. African-American business ventures are at a disadvantage because African-American economic behavioral patterns are adversely affected by a psychological dynamic that values light skin tone. This problem will be resolved only with an education process that will inform the community of its origin and teach in its place the moral value of financial self-discipline grounded in self-love. Self-love leads to financial responsibility and self-discipline. They both perpetuate behavior patterns that enhance common community progress, and individual self-interest.

## Financial Dysfunction: Budgeting, Saving, Investing, Maintaining a Good Credit Standing

African Americans' financial dysfunction is rooted in their oppression in the U.S. This is perhaps the dilemma of the human spirit, when downtrodden individuals utilize too much of their financial resources in an attempt to ease inner pain, and to acquire a social image of dignity and worth in the eyes of others. This reaction is a bid to gain a sense of acceptance and self-worth. In fact, this financial behavior pattern started soon after African Americans left the plantations as freed persons. However, today the problem of spending beyond one's means is a serious one and cannot be solely attributed to present-day oppression. Despite post-slavery economic, political, and social oppression many African Americans have made some tremendous financial gains. At the same time, financial progress remains problematic for many more African Americans. The economic challenge for the African-American community is to utilize its financial earnings as resources to obtain economic power. As mentioned above, African-American unemployment has dropped during the 1990s, but it is still a concern because it remains too high. Making one's money grow is of vast importance to the African-American family and community; making one's money grow has an indelible influence upon economic empowerment in the African American community.

In his book, *Black Lies, White Lies, The Truth According to Tony Brown*, Brown concludes that "Black Americans now earn nearly $500 billion annually."[91] Furthermore, Brown states, "and yet Blacks spend only 3 percent of their income with a Black business or Black professional. By spending 97 percent of their money outside of their racial community, they exacerbate their social and economic problems."[92] Brown makes an important point, but at the root of the issue of self-help is a more fundamental problem, over spending; it ultimately prevents financial progress, and the responsible management of one's personal financial affairs. Financial dysfunction involves spending that exceeds financial means. It is a spending pattern that functions to ease inner pain, fill an inner gap in an effort to find peace, dignity, and meaning. This dysfunction stems from social rejection and other forms of oppression. The spender seeks comfort from external things rather than his or her own internal spiritual powers. Financial dysfunction leaves its victims vulnerable to making sound and self-loving choices. Why? Because under the influence of certain external powers, victims give more credibility to things than they will to their internal spiritual power innately created in all humanity by God. They come to believe that these are the things that will make them feel complete, fill this inner gap in their soul, and give sustained personal meaning and self-worth. In these instances, the real problem is a lack of self-love and the tendency to adopt a definition of self imposed by these external social powers. When one surrenders to this self-defeating dynamic one gives up one's own spiritual powers in exchange for the illusion of personal power, but actually this person becomes even more powerless. Too much influence and credibility given to external social powers preempts one of one's authentic spiritual powers, and personal choices are contingent upon the latest fade or some other external social thing. Financial dysfunction takes place when one is rendered powerless to tap into one's reservoir of spiritual powers; it does not take from an individual the deep urge to gain a sense of somebodiness. The pain and insecurity at the root of this need seek for relief through an attempt to gain a sense of somebodiness, and in fact, are best described as a hole, void, or gap that person attempts to fill. Indeed, when this gap is filled with anything other than spiritual nurture, which is an indication of self-love, dysfunction and destructive behavioral patterns will be the result. The attempt to gain a sense of somebodiness is a positive and loving impulse when its source is the internal spirit powers given to humanity by God, which are love, faith, peace, prayer, and hope; these are the resources necessary for ultimate human purpose and spiritual meaning.

Financial training to develop skills in the areas of budgeting, saving, investing, and the maintenance of a good credit standing would aid in deterring destructive spending behavior patterns. However, the need for validation from others can stimulate this behavior again, and self-love is the only remedy that will destroy this need. Africans-Americans no longer need to ease inner pain by overspending in order to gain a sense of human dignity and a sense of acceptance. It is crucial to the effectiveness of this training that it is spiritually structured in African-American religious institutions; they must take seriously the fact the personality formation of African-Americans took shape in a society that perpetuated in them self-doubt and insecurity. In fact, some cultural symbols in U.S. society still transmit messages of self-doubt and insecurity to the African-American psyche. For example, the image of Christ as a white male and the white standard of beauty are seen daily in the media and other settings in the U.S.

In fact, the historic economic reality of African Americans was oppressive and bleak to say the least; low wages and the lack of financial opportunities made saving next to impossible. Many families could identify with the old adage, rob Peter to pay Paul, because they lived it. The network for human development, the leadership at the center of African-American culture, taught that dress had much to do with gaining a sense of dignity. It influenced first and lasting impressions of an individual and a family. For example, parents would spend money to purchase school clothes for their children to sustain family dignity, even if the money was needed to pay a major debt. Parents often interpreted their social reputation through their children; their children's social manners, dress, and image were connected to family dignity, reputation, and image. Human dignity came first, and it often was too expensive. African Americans set forth to prove their human worth to the external world rather than just accept it; this was in response to a society that stigmatized and treated African Americans as less than human. Personal power was often lost to external powers and African Americans allowed external powers to have excessive influence on their definition of self. In addition, parents were presented with situations where the choice was to buy a book for school or food for the family. Food was the logical and overwhelming choice. Financial conditions such as these were a fact of life, and this meant that educational hopes and dreams were placed on the back burner. Some children had to work for the family rather than attend school. These were all difficult choices, but funds were limited and this made budgeting virtually impossible. In fact, not budgeting grew from these types of situations. The culture did not want individuals from the community to be perceived as persons without dignity, and dress was important to this outcome.

It is significant that securing human dignity and self-worth were directly related to appearance, family, and self-pride, and social impression. This reflected whether one's image and reputation made one's family and community proud of him or her or not. This dynamic was connected to spending patterns. Often one spent beyond one's means to obtain and maintain a perception of sombodiness. Many pastors of African-American churches drove expensive automobiles such as the Cadillac, Buick, and Oldsmobile. In fact, many of their congregations prided themselves in this fact. This was because they gained a sense of pride and worth by being associated with this type of prosperity, and having a leader of dignity, respectability, and accomplishment. This was the type of leader that made African-Americans proud. African-American pastors and church leaders were spokes persons for their community, and had to present themselves and their community to the larger society with respect and credibility. Indeed, their level of education, their dress, and the overall impression they made had a direct impact upon the perception of the African-American community. Traditionally, church affiliation carried with it certain positive or negative social and economic associations. Perceptions with regard to church and family reputation were powerful and very real in the African American experience.

Financial dysfunction cannot be dealt with unless there is a clear understanding of the economic, political, and social conditions from which it derived. In fact, this dysfunction stems from years of oppression and is the root cause of this overwhelming internal conflict that perpetuates the tendency to overspend in order to establish a sense of self-worth. This dysfunction is basically a psychological struggle and attempt to exist with and to ease this internal pain. Historically, African-Americans' struggle for dignity in the U.S. has had a direct impact on the development of financial skills, and specifically with regard to handling personal finances. Since Marcus Garvey Movement that started in Harlem in 1919, teaching financial skills and economic development for the establishment of self-reliance have never been the primary focus of any civil rights agenda in African-American community. Garvey's approach to obtain liberation was through education and self-reliance. African-American civil rights leaders focused on winning the vote to gain political equality, and on education to obtain social change. In fact, the focus for the African-American community during the Civil Rights Movements of the 1960s and 1970s and even the post Civil Rights Movement years has been political and social equality. Undoubtedly, some attention was given to economic development and assistance, but the primary focus was on issues such as voting rights, unemployment, equal education, and etc. The Poor Peoples Campaign of the early 1970s that was led by the SCLC was a demonstration to secure from Congress an Economic Bill of Rights for the Disadvantaged Poor; it set forth to guarantee a job to all. This campaign was not a movement with an economic plan for the African-American community in the Garvey tradition of self-reliance. Although some African Americans have excellent financial skills, many do not. In fact, this is one of the important points of Brown's position stated above. The tendency to live above one's financial means is a widespread cultural problem in the U.S. African-Americans just can not afford to continue to join the party. Over the course of 137 years since President Lincoln signed the Emancipation Proclamation in 1863, African Americans have been preoccupied with securing basic human rights and dignity, and for good reason. The emphasis has not been on money; even education, as was mentioned earlier in Chapter 7, was pursued for other reasons such as respect, personal and community pride, dignity, and acceptance by European Americans. However, African American youths at risk as well as others must be taught financial skills so they will be empowered to take control their own financial future.

Currently, one-half of American households have investments in the U.S. stock market. The path that leads to financial stability is simple: budgeting, maintaining of a good credit standing, saving, and investing. The following are essential beginning steps necessary for sound financial management. They are:

Establish a financial plan to accomplish the following long-term goals:

1. Establish a long-term personal vision with short-term goals to include:

    a. establish educational goals

b. obtain financial assistance for education
c. set time line for accomplishing educational goals
d. seek the advice of a career planner and do research on careers
e. focus on ways and means to further career development
f. assess desired earning potential
g. set a time line for marriage and starting a family to prevent premature events from interfering with goals
h. find a mentor to get help, suggestions, feedback, and inspiration in order to bring personal vision to fruition

2. Seek the advice of a financial counselor

3. Structure long-term and short-term financial goals utilizing present income to:

   a. establish a long-term vision for obtaining wealth
   b. establish a budget
   c. adopt a disciplined and frugal lifestyle, living by the standards established by your budget
   d. educate yourself by reading books, magazines, and other publications on financial matters and the tax system; pay off all debts; with the exception of a house mortgage, adopt the principle of debt free living; learn the different ways that mortgages may be paid off years early and implement in your budget when the time is right
   e. pay yourself in the form of savings and investments
   f. save for retirement by establishing a Roth IRA, and invest in no-load mutual funds and bonds rather than in traditional savings accounts to maximize your investment returns
   g. monitor credit standing
   h. live below your means
   i. establish a pattern of giving to your church

The following are common financial pitfalls that will prevent financial success:

1. Spending without discipline and a financial plan defined from your personal vision; spending without a focused budget that includes saving and investing.

2. Housing: renting or buying a home that exceeds one's financial means is a major problem; a high expenditure in this area can result in serious financial problems because it is typically the biggest expense. A good rule is not to allow housing expenses to exceed 30 percent of one's income. For a single person just beginning a career, the most affordable housing, such as renting a room, is the best option; it will allow one to live below one's means and allow savings and investing.

3. Transportation: If one cannot comfortably afford it, one should not buy a new vehicle; one should purchase a used vehicle without going into debt. This will keep a significant portion of one's income free for savings and investing.

4. The following are programs that churches and mosques may use as tools to educate youths at risk and the African-American community as a whole:

   a. The Stock Market Game. Contact the Rainbow/PUSH Coalition to get information on an educational initiative entitled, the Stock Market Game. In their book, *It's About the MONEY!* Rev. Jesse L. Jackson, Sr., and Jesse L. Jackson, Jr., outline the curriculum and structure of this initiative; indeed they maintain that it has empowered some youths. According to them, 25 children associated with Rainbow/PUSH have gained significant knowledge about the stock market and are beginning to utilize their newly learned skills as tools to form a personal investment strategy. An educational program of this nature in African-American churches and mosques has the potential to teach thousands of youths at risk and parents with little knowledge of the stock market skills and tools that will change their lives and give them new financial hope.[93]

   b. Coupons for Groceries. This is a program that has the potential to save a family hundreds of dollars each month. The funds saved from grocery shopping may be utilized to get out of debt and invest. A family of 4 has the potential to save two to four hundred dollars monthly by actively using coupons. Large companies such as Best Foods, Proctor and Gamble, and Johnson and Johnson give free samples of products and coupons that may result in great savings for a family to use to shape a better economic future. Accumulating coupons can become a hobby that fosters good spending habits; it will teach discipline, sacrifice, independence, and most of all the importance of being frugal. This is a simple strategy a family can use with just creativity and determination. It is important to remember to create a system that works best for oneself.

c. In-sourcing. Learn who the people capable of providing valuable services in your community are; they are resources with talents, who can be a financial benefit to the community. For example, dentists, auto mechanics, accountants, lawyers, medical doctors, nurses, carpenters, plumbers may be willing to offer services that will save families funds and educate them as well. After establishing this type of program, set up specific times that these services will be provided to church and mosque members.

d. Community Resource Pooling. This is an economic-development program that will benefit individuals, families, churches, and mosques, as well as the community. Pooling individual financial resources to make larger investments will give a better financial future for those willing to make the sacrifices. Indeed, many dreams would be realized in this type of business relationship. The alternatives are to save or to seek a loan; both may be difficult. Persons and institutions who have similar dreams, ambitions, interests, and goals can set the legal guidelines and parameters to govern this association, establish the business structure, create a vision statement, and form their own investment association to make money and to accomplish financial goals. Community resource pooling is different in the sense that members will make money with a team of other investors rather than alone. The fact that many individuals, families, and churches can potentially get involved in a business relationship of this nature and magnitude means that many can benefit from such a strategy. This is a plan for dreamers. With a vision and hard work, financial independence may be imminent. This type of economic- development program is a strategy for building community. Historically, many immigrant families and individuals have used this program to gain economic power; some have been successful.

e. Career Center. The primary function of such a center housed in a local church or mosque will be to provide informational resources that will assist youths and others in obtaining employment, training, career advancement, and preparation for college entrance and other exams.

(1) Job openings. The focus is to improve quality of life through job placement. Establish a right to work campaign involving local employers to include government entities and companies agreeing to bring down unemployment in the community. Maintain an employment placement list at the church. These employers' job listings will be submitted to the church through a mutual agreement. An agreement that specifies that both parties agree and consent to jobs being filled after prospective employees complete a basic training course sponsored and taught by the church. An agreement of this nature will provide employers hiring stability and jobs for the unemployed of the community.

(2) Employment Basic Training Course. It will help trainees with resume preparation. A Career Specialist will teach trainees how to use career center computers to write and update outstanding resumes. The Career Specialist will teach trainees job interview skills that focus on social skills, speech, questions to ask and not to ask, letters of recommendation, and dress. After the job is obtained the Career Specialist will teach trainees job etiquette, including the importance of work attendance and punctuality, attitude and social skills, dress and grooming standards, and how to be savvy with regards to career progression. The section on career progression will teach the connection between personal ambition and work place motivation and the need to display interest in the job and in the business' overall operation and vision.

Youths Investment Training. In their book, *Its About The MONEY!*, Rev. Jesse Jackson, Sr., and Jesse Jackson, Jr., give information on two curriculums that are educating youths. These programs are offered in the summer and mini-models of these should be utilized by the African-American church and mosque to teach youths about money management, the stock market, and the U.S. and global financial systems. According to father and son, the state of Wisconsin's Youth Enterprise Academy sponsors a ten-day summer program for ninth and tenth grade students at the University of Wisconsin's Milwaukee campus; it gives extensive instructions to these youths on the basics of economics and capitalism.

> The course covers how the stock market works, the credit market, personal finance, savings, and investing to mention a few areas of concentration. The other program to teach youths is The Bull and Bear Investment. It meets every July in Kansas City, Missouri, and is conducted by Douglas Coe. Mr. Coe is president and chief executive officer of Moody Reid Inc., a local investment firm in Kansas City Missouri. Coe started the camp in 1994 to educate inner city youths to the investment world. His idea came when he noticed that during the summers sports training camps dominated youths activities; they trained the body, but he started Bull and Bear Investment Camp to train the mind. Students who complete the course receive $500.00 in U.S. savings bonds. It is an excellent program that needs to be conducted on a national level. These youths participate in a mock stock market, role-playing sessions that simulate labor-management talks, and are taught on a wide range of subjects in the area of savings and investing.[94]

Youths at risk aspire to obtain the good life, but before they gain the skills, tools, and resources to fulfill the American dream, they often lose all hope; when they acquire the Destructive Capitalistic Personality Complex (DCPC) their lives will never be the same. They must learn basic life skills, and in order for Black Theology to establish meaning and relevance with these youths, it must speak to the risks that they face and offer alternatives. The above management plan for success is a starting point for the African-American church to educate youths at risk. Youths at risk must be taught to think for the long-term rather than for the short term; short-term thinking contributes to the overall problem to youths at risk becoming vulnerable to acquiring the DCPC. Furthermore, short-term thinking is devoid of a vision for the future; it employs short-term means to gain success that may include illegal shortcuts. It seeks instant gratification rather than lasting means for long-term rewards. Long-term commitment and effort are unattractive to youths at risk because they cannot envision them. With this blindness or lack of vision to the future, they become willing to sacrifice their lives and freedom to gain a short lived sensation of respectability, economic power, and social gratification. Without long-term vision, youths at risk have no motive to prepare themselves for legitimate employment and a life of meaning. Short-term thinking of this nature is guided by the same external powers mentioned above rather than by internal spiritual powers. Patience as an essential spiritual value and a tool necessary to live a meaningful life is not recognized by the short-term thinking of youths at risk; they want instant success that under normal circumstances would take most persons years to obtain. We must teach youths at risk to

1. Think on a long-term basis.
2. Adopt a long-term personal vision.
3. Envision a successful image of themselves in the future.
4. Use their internal spiritual powers to find discipline, patience, and self-love, rather than being controlled by external powers that will ultimately destroy them.
5. Utilize the educational and economical resources available to them as U.S. citizens to accomplish long-term goals.
6. Learn basic life skills necessary for becoming successful and productive citizens in the African-American community and in U.S. society.
7. Learn the necessity to become personally innovative, resourceful, and savvy in order to realize their dream.

As mentioned above, historically the majority of the leadership of the African-American community placed more emphasis upon integration as the route to obtain self-worth and dignity. Less emphasis was placed upon inculcating in individuals the personal management and basic life skills necessary to function competitively in a fully integrated society and economy. The plan outlined above is a point of departure that will lead youths at risk into a more meaningful, moral, and rewarding course in life; it will provide the structure necessary to help youths at risk escape the DCPC.

According to present-day standards, a lack of financial discipline is a serious problem in relation to budgeting, saving, and investing. The lack of financial discipline may extend to a lack of discipline and sense of responsibility in other significant areas of one's life. The failure to practice discipline in the many other areas of one's life fosters a deep sense of failure that will ultimately make one feel miserably trapped in a life defined by one's own choices. Such despair and resent will exist until there is total acceptance of responsibility for one's own life. This simple lack of discipline can be very problematic for youths at risk if it is not resolved during those early impressionable years of their development; it can potentially lead them toward even more destructive behaviors and to a total breakdown of their morality.

This is what occurs when the DCPC is acquired, and at this point, one has destroyed one's own hope. In all fairness, there are other complex issues and circumstances that influence individual outcome in many instances; they are factors in the historical oppression in the U.S. Lack of discipline is a key reason for the lack of success among some African-Americans, and the DCPC has exacerbated despair. A self-reliant African-American community is the hope for the future. However, for self-reliance to become a reality, it will require a disciplined African-American community energized with the same determination and conviction that existed during the successful Montgomery Bus Boycott in the 1950s. For self-reliance to develop, there must be discipline along with conviction in the areas of budgeting, saving, and investing. I am not suggesting that the external social powers of racism were not the overwhelming cause of the economic misfortunes of African Americans. To the contrary, years of racism and oppression created the self-doubt and internal conflict within the African-American psyche.

## Spiritual Values Necessary for Self-Reliance

Earlier in this chapter, I discussed the origins of the principles of spiritual awareness, education, community responsibility, family responsibility, and vocational responsibility. I pointed out that they were developed within African Americans as a result of a community structure and a process of human development. This structure no longer remains in the African-American community, and a new structure must be established in order to restore those same values, which are useful for strengthening the character of youths at risk. Youths at risk need to adopt these spiritual principles in order for the African-American community to resolve its problem of widespread nihilism and start the development of a self-reliant community. I have described in detail the practical mechanisms responsible for the establishment of the process of human development, which operated in the African-American community to shape spiritual values within the family and community. However, there are several other significant values that did not play a role in that process of human development, but are necessary for youths at risk and their attainment of self-reliance.

In order for a community to become self-reliant it must focus on its vulnerabilities and turn them into strengths. Historically, the African-American community has been rich in spirituality, but in the last three decades an entire generation of youths grew up somewhat isolated from this rich spiritual tradition. In fact, there is a noticeable breakdown in the spiritual and moral development of youths at risk, which is reflected in high crime rates. This is the area in which the African-American community is most vulnerable; we stand to lose not only these youths, but also some of the gains made since slavery. This loss may happen due to a lack of interest and participation in community affairs. The false value of materialism through any means necessary has become deadly for youths at risk. This problem is directly related to the issues of self-love, self-esteem, self-discipline, spiritual awareness, family and community responsibility, and education. Historically, the African-American community has not utilized its financial resources to its full advantage. Financial responsibility is another vulnerable area that must be turned into a strength. This would be a responsible move toward the establishment of self-reliance.

**Self-Love**

Spiritual awareness is directly related to one's love and nurture of one's self. I mentioned earlier that the first step in the healing process to prevent youths at risk from acquiring the DCPC is spiritual awareness. Many psychologists have concluded that self-love is necessary to be able to love another human being. One cannot love someone else if one does not first love oneself. The so-called loyalty shared among gang members is destructive; they claim that their deep sense of loyalty for each other is grounded in love. However, their notions of love and loyalty only lead to destruction; they are both illusions grounded in destructive behavioral tendencies that will ultimately return the same destruction to them that they have sent out into the universe. In fact, this principle is called the law of sowing and reaping from the Christian perspective, and karma from the Buddhist perspective.

Spiritual awareness enriches one's self-image and self-worth; it enables one to arrive at a deeper understanding of one's purpose and character. Spiritual awareness aids one's ability to work through the complex challenges that arise in the course of life; it initiates a developmental process of spiritual growth through self-nurturing. This ability to nurture oneself reflects a healthy spiritual encountering of oneself; a spiritual validation of oneself has taken place. Spiritual awareness provides meaning and purpose in one's life because it enables one to learn the meaning of life itself. The Christian faith teaches that one's love for God and neighbor is directly connected with self-love. Jesus' love command is the central theme and is at the core to the true meaning of Christianity. It reads, "... Thou shall love the Lord thy God with all thy heart, and with all thy soul, and with all thy strength, and with thy mind; and thy neighbor as thyself."[95] The lawyer with whom Jesus was speaking in verse 29 asked Jesus, "but who is my neighbor?" The question reveals his lack of spiritual awareness due to his obvious attempt to manipulate Jesus and his inability to understand that love in this context required one to give totally of oneself to provide for the needs of one's neighbor. Love in this case is one's willingness to provide for any person in need. Spiritual awareness is an indication that a nurturing process is taking place within one's self.

Spiritual nurturing is a component of self-love; it is a process that never ends in the course of one's life and leads to growth. This spiritual transformational process is the first step toward self-love. This process will bring youths to a deep spiritual awareness that will cultivate self-nurturing, increase understanding of one's personality, enrich one's self-image, and enhance one's ability to love oneself. Furthermore, when youths at risk embrace self-love they will no longer view themselves as victims. The elimination of the victim mentality is the first indication that spiritual growth has taken place and a reverence for God realized; youths at risk perception of life will no longer be viewed as in a struggle for meaning against the community, society, and the universe. Instead, they will become at one with their community, society, and the universe. To learn compassion and a sense of responsibility to make the world better, one must look at the world through a spiritual lens. Without it one will have a distorted view of the world and its people. The development of self-love among youths at risk is a necessary step toward the establishment of a self-reliant African-American community; becoming self-reliant is the true meaning of liberation for the African-American community, and nothing else will suffice. In fact, this type of spiritual growth will empower them to look beyond their blackness in become one with God and the universe.

Self-reliance is an obtainable goal. In making self-reliance a reality, the crucial challenge is to end the destructive cycles of crime, drug use, gang activity, and violence in the African-American community. These activities are committed by African-American youths with the DCPC. Many more youths are at risk of acquiring the DCPC because they are growing up in nihilistic social environments. The African-American community is in a major spiritual and moral crisis. These youths must be transformed with the spiritual principles mentioned above so that they will become a productive part of the solution, and contribute to the establishment of a self-reliant African-American community. Spiritual values are the substance and means necessary to empower youths at risk to lead responsible, moral lives. Their behavior patterns will become productive rather than destructive, making them part of the solution rather than part of the problem. Spiritual values lead to responsible behavior. The two principles of spiritual awareness and self-love are essential to the development of a self-reliant African-American community. The spiritual values of family responsibility, community responsibility, and vocational responsibility as described earlier are not accessible unless one develops self-love. Before the end of segregation as a principle, these values were made available in the major institutions of the African-American community, the family, the church, and the schools. These values were transmitted to individuals by family members, ministers, teachers, and community mentors. This was the structure that provided a process of human spiritual and moral development.

This structure that aided human development must be reestablished in order for these values to be transmitted to youths at risk. It will be impossible for the African-American community to eliminate the DCPC and gain self-reliance without transforming youths at risk; these values are significant for a spiritual transformation of this nature. They will provide the substance for personal power, which includes integrity and a personal commitment to improve oneself and one's community. The first step is to develop spiritual awareness because it will cultivate self-love. One cannot adopt the other essential values of family, community, and vocational responsibility without first developing self-love. Furthermore, the most important element in this healing process is the development of self-love.

The spiritual value of self-love in the African-American context is necessary to accomplish self-reliance. Self-destructive behavior patterns grew out of a negative and distorted sense of self. Therefore, self-love is the necessary value for obtaining a positive sense of self. Self-love in this context is defined from the Afrocentric perspective mentioned earlier. That is, it is intrinsically linked to a sense of community belonging and to the attainment of community self-interest. The principles of self-discipline, self-determination, and self-confidence must grow out of this Afrocentric notion of self-love if self-destructive behavior patterns are not to develop. Therefore, self-confidence, self-discipline, and self-determination as spiritual principles, are discussed here from an Afrocentric perspective, and self-love is a given. Self-love is necessary for the development of self-confidence, self-determination, and self-discipline.

Meaning and purpose in one's life, from the Afrocentric perspective, are by-products of self-love. This moves one from merely drifting in a meaningless existence in which one is vulnerable to being shaped by external powers to living a life of meaning in which one obtains spiritual and personal powers, including vision and focus. This is the essence of the spiritual and moral dilemma where youths at risk become vulnerable to acquire the DCPC. Youths at risk are merely existing without meaning and purpose in a nihilistic social world and are shaped by the external powers of their social environment. The spiritual principles outlined in this chapter will provide youths at risk with the substance to obtain spiritual and personal powers. Additionally, these principles will at the same time strengthen the African-American community with the inner power that will enable it to determine its own destiny of self-reliance rather than remaining vulnerable to the external powers of nihilism. Subsequently are listed concise definitions of the essential spiritual and moral values mentioned above to establish an understanding of the practical application of each in the African-American struggle:

1. Spiritual Awareness: It is the spiritual substance necessary to start the healing process for youths at risk of acquiring the DCPC. It is the spiritual substance that will change one's worldview and belief system, awakens one's spirit, resolve any inner conflict, and bring one to a deeper knowledge of self and to a oneness with God and the universe. It will establish one's faith. It will provide one with spiritual principles that lay a foundation for moral development. It will provide structure to one's life and a moral code one needs to govern one's life. It is a process of self-nurturing that leads to growth.

2. Education: In the African-American experience education as a principle is defined from an Afrocentric perspective. Education functioned as a moral principle in the sense that it prepared African Americans to participate in a meaningful way in the Afrocentric community approach to accomplishing individual, family, and community liberation. Education was viewed as essential for the development of individual, family, and community dignity, and this understanding of education was taught in schools and churches throughout the African-American community. Education as a moral principle from an Afrocentric perspective holds that one must become educated not only for one's own self-improvement, but to help the community overcome ignorance and poverty. Also, it was a necessity to provide moral leadership in the institutions for community

development in the effort to fight oppression and further the cause of liberation. It establishes professional meaning and self-worth that enable one to assume family and community responsibility. It broadens one's intellectual awareness and functions as a means to cultivate character.

3. Self-love: Self-destructive behavior patterns grew out of the lack of self-love. Self-love is defined from an Afrocentric perspective and is applicable in this context. Self-love enables one to form a positive sense of self and overcome the negative self-image engrained in African-Americans' personality during slavery and post slavery-oppression. Self-love is intrinsically linked to the pursuit of community self-interest. It leads one to an intimate process of spiritual nurturing that leads to finding meaning and purpose; it cultivates personal power and equips one with the inner substance to assist the community.

4. Self-confidence: Faith in one's abilities. It allows one to have the ability to establish a vision, devise a plan, and pursue that plan. It grows out of self-love; it develops an ego grounded in one's spiritual convictions.

5. Self-determination: From an Afrocentric perspective, the will and inner strength to chart a path. It grows out of self-love.

6. Self-discipline: The willpower and focus to make sacrifices in order to accomplish individual and community goals.

7. Responsibility: An ethical principle, grounded in spirituality, that guides conduct toward the accomplishment of individual, family, and community goals in the African-American experience.

8. Community Responsibility: In the Afrocentric perspective, the duty to work for justice on behalf of the community. An obligation to work for the moral and spiritual development of the individual, family, and community.

9. Family Responsibility: The duty to support family life and

development, and to uphold the moral standards and reputation of the family within the community.

10. Afrocentrism: The worldview informed by African culture that promotes a community approach to individual and community development. It functions as a collective approach to attaining liberation.

## Conclusion

Youths at risk are in a moral crisis, and the solution is to plant in them the spiritual principles outlined in this chapter. This crisis is spiritual in nature, and this is why I propose the reestablishment of a process of human spiritual development through the Christian church and the Muslim mosque within the African-American community. I have suggested values rooted in Afrocentrism, which I believe youths at risk will respond to. This approach echoes the African proverb that says that it takes a village to raise a child. Widespread nihilism will continue to influence the personality formation of African-American youths unless the African-American community organizes its collective energy and fights it as it fought injustice in the 1960s and 1970s. If it fails to devise a plan to do this, youths at risk will eventually acquire the Destructive Capitalist Personality Complex (DCPC). Furthermore, the destructive cycle of violence, crime, gang activity, and drugs will remain their chosen path to material gain and a sense of self-worth. These activities will perpetuate family brokenness, disinterest in education, unemployment, and incarceration.

Spiritual awareness is the first priority because it will lead youths at risk to see the world through a self-liberating lens that will provide a fundamental structure for moral self-examination to take place. As aforementioned, spiritual awareness is the fertile ground from which the spiritual and moral principles outlined in this book will grow. In order for one's behavior to change, one's fundamental values must first change. Spiritual awareness initiates a process of self-examination that will bring youths at risk to self-dissatisfaction, then to self-evaluation, and finally to a deep sense of spiritual self-realization. Acquiring spiritual awareness is the point of departure into a spiritual process to obtain the moral principles that will radically change one's life from self-destructiveness to constructiveness. These principles are most crucial to put youths at risk in touch with a spiritual aspect of themselves that they had been unaware of. The primary function of this spiritual self will be an inner guide or coach accessible for making moral daily choices.

African-American churches and mosques are the primary institutions for this healing process. They have been the traditional organizations for social transformation and the key providers of leadership in the African-American community, and their roles in this process are crucial. The challenge in cultivating these spiritual principles in youths at risk will be to bring them to the point where they are open to spiritual learning; they must become dissatisfied with their life and arrive at the point where they yearn for a better alternative. Spiritual awareness brings them to this point, but the process of human moral and spiritual development through relatives, teachers, ministers, and mentors also brings them to the point where they desire healing. Many individuals do not reach this point until they experience some type of pain that overwhelms them and makes them see everything in a new light. Malcolm X's time in prison brought him to the point of self-dissatisfaction. He began to look for a better way of living, which for him was centered on spirituality. He went through a transformational crisis. A transformational crisis is one in which one's worldview is radically changed. In the case of an individual with the DCPC, a transformational crisis may occur when that person faces the consequences of his or her destructive behavior.

C. S. Lewis in many of his writings suggests that life is the greatest teacher because it puts pain in our lives, which is what spurs us to grow spiritually; he described this as God being a sculptor perfecting us with the blows of His chisel. When an individual goes through a valley experience it brings him or her to the point of self-evaluation, which leads a person to change his or her life. Pain is traumatic, but it brings with it the potential for spiritual growth. Youths with the DCPC are already in deep pain; an overwhelming trauma could lead to spiritual awareness. Self-reflection takes place and produces self-dissatisfaction. The painful experience brings them to the knowledge that their lifestyles make them vulnerable to ultimate destruction. Spiritual awareness leads to this realization. However, this is not to suggest that the only way youths with the DCPC can reach spiritual awareness is through a valley experience. As previously mentioned, they can obtain it through the process of human moral and spiritual development, which has been a traditional element in the African-American community.

These principles are obtainable, and we owe it to youths at risk to make them accessible in environments that are not Afrocentric in nature. Indeed, they may be made accessible through education. School systems can accommodate this process in classroom settings by teaching courses that will define and discuss the DCPC from a sociological and spiritual perspective. A course entitled "Youths At Risk: Defeating the Odds and Becoming Productive Citizens in the U.S." will reach some. The goal of this educational device will be to cultivate these moral principles in youths by engaging youths at risk in any of the settings mentioned below. To remain within the legal guidelines for the separation of church and state, this course can be sponsored by African-American churches, mosques, and community organizations and taught at schools, churches, mosques, or community centers on the weekends. This book can be utilized as a guide to teach it. Additionally, institutions such as the YMCA and boys' and girls' clubs can be invaluable in teaching these principles. As previously suggested, civil rights organizations can sponsor spiritual crusades and rallies modeled on the Million Man March in communities across this nation to educate youths at risk and others about the self-defeating DCPC and how it can be defeated.

# Notes

## Chapter 1

1 James H. Cone's Black Theology sets forth to address the problem of African-American oppression in the U.S.; for Cone racism in the U.S. is clearly the cause of African-American oppression. Cited in James H. Cone, *Black Theology and Black Power*, (Seabury Press 1970, preface). There is a consistent charge in Cone's Black Theology that racism is the primary enemy with respect to African-American oppression in the U.S. In the 1970 preface cited above, Cone maintains, "in a society where persons are oppressed because they are black, Christian theology must become black theology." Indeed, oppression that becomes widespread in society and is a social reality because of race or color is clearly racism; this is absolutely the case in the African-American experience in the U.S. and Cone's Black Theology is based on this fact. In the above statement, Cone is clearly referring to racism. This is a consistent position of Cone's and is a theme at the center of his writings for and in support of Black Theology as being necessary in light of African-American oppression in the U.S. The question is why Christian theology must become Black theology? Cone's response is that it must become a theology that is "unreservedly identified with the goals of the oppressed and seeks to interpret the divine character of their struggle for liberation." In fact, Cone is clearly utilizing Black theology to address the problem of racism, and he views racism as the enemy and the perpetrator of African-American oppression. In this same work in 1970, *Black Theology and Black Power*, Black Theology is presented as a new theological insight; it is a solution to African-American oppression. For Cone, Black Power is not only a theological response to the racism that is at the core of Christianity, but is a social and political response to racism in U.S. society; it is a unified black response to a society that uses racism to distort true Christian theology (Black Theology) and to justify the oppression of African American in U.S. society. For Cone Black Theology is Black Power, and they are intertwined as theological insight and community action against racism.

2 These essays were published in 1972 and government of South Africa responded to them as though they posed an immediate threat to apartheid, a way of life that granted the white minority economic, political, and social advantage over its black majority. These essays help to put in place a Black South African Theology that called for the elimination of apartheid and for Black majority rule of the government; the struggle to maintain political and economic power and to take those powers caused the social unrest to intensify. The writers of these essays became the targets of the government's tactics of intimidation and retribution in an effort to maintain good order and discipline, and the keep the Black Theology message from becoming accessible to Black South Africans. Cited in Preface by Basil Moore, ed., comp., *The Challenge of Black Theology in South Africa (*Atlanta: John Knox Press, 1973), viii.

3 Basil Moore, "What Is Black Theology?" in *The Challenge of Black Theology in South Africa (*Atlanta: John Knox Press, 1973), 1.

4 Moore, editor's preface to *The Challenge Of Black Theology,* vii.

5 Moore, editor's preface to *The Challenge of Black Theology,* viii.

6 Moore, editor's preface to *The Challenge of Black Theology,* ix.

7 Moore, editor's preface to *The Challenge of Black Theology,* ix.

8 Steve Biko, *"Black Consciousness and the Quest for a True Humanity"* in *The Challenge of Black Theology in South Africa,* comp. Basil Moore (Atlanta: John Knox Press, 1973), 39.

9 Biko, 39.

10 Moore, "What Is Black Theology?" in *The Challenge of Black Theology in South Africa,* comp. Basil Moore (Atlanta: John Knox Press, 1973), 39.

11 Cone's theology was initially presented with the publication of *Black Theology and Black Power* (San Francisco: Harper & Row, 1969).

12 Noel Leo Erskine, *King among the Theologians* (Cleveland: Pilgrim Press, 1994), 85.

13 Erskine, 85.

14 Ralph Abernathy, *And the Walls Came Tumbling Down: Ralph David Abernathy—An Autobiography* (New York: Harper & Row, 1989), 456.

15 In Abernathy's autobiography, *And the Walls Came Tumbling Down,* he asserts that nonviolent direct action was a strategy grounded in the theology of suffering from the Christian perspective (p. 157). This was a belief that he practiced until his death in April, 1990. As evidenced by their actions, the followers of King continued to believe in nonviolent direct action rather than Cone's thought on Black power. Throughout the 1960s, 1970s, and 1980s numerous organizations, including Operation People United to Serve Humanity (Operation PUSH), the Southern Christian leadership Conference (SCLC), and the National Association for the Advancement of Colored People (NAACP), held the nonviolent marches and protests advocated by King's philosophy.

16 James Cone, *A Black Theology of Liberation,* 2nd ed. (Maryknoll, N.Y.: Orbis Books, 1986), 130.

17 Erskine, 92.

18 Cone, *Black Theology of Liberation*, 8–9.

19 Cone, *Black Theology of Liberation*, 8–9.

20 Cone, *Black Theology of Liberation*, 9.

21 Harry A. Ploski and James Williams, eds., *The Negro Almanac: A Reference Work on the African American*, 5th ed. (New York: Gale Research, 1989), 1507.

## Chapter 2

22 Cornel West, *Race Matters* (Boston: Beacon Press, 1993), 14–15.

23 Deborah Prothrow-Stith and Michaele Weissman, *Deadly Consequences* (New York: Harper Perenial, 1991), 6.

24 Prothrow-Stith and Weissman, 6.

25 Prothrow-Stith and Weissman, 6.

26 Prothrow-Stith and Weissman, 2.

27 Prothrow-Stith and Weissman, xvii.

28 Prothrow-Stith and Weissman, 111.

29 Prothrow-Stith and Weissman, 113.

30 Prothrow-Stith and Weissman, 111.

31 Louise L. Hornor, ed., *Black Americans: A Statistical Sourcebook* (Palo Alto, Calif.: Information Publications, 1994), 184–87.

## Chapter 3

32 George Cummings, *A Common Journey: Black Theology (USA) and Latin American Liberation Theology* (Maryknoll, N.Y.: Orbis Books, 1993), 1.

33 Cummings, 3.

34 Quoted in Garth Baker-Fletcher, *Xodus: An African American Male Journey* (Minneapolis: Fortress Press, 1996), 52.

35 James Cone, *God of the Oppressed* (New York: Seabury Press, 1975), 154.

36 Cone, *God of the Oppressed*, 154.

37 Martin Luther King, Jr., *Why We Can't Wait* (New York: New American Library, 1964), 77.

38 Luther Ivory, "Martin Luther King, Jr. as a Theologian of Radical Involvement" (Ph.D. diss., Emory University, 1996), 5.

39 Cummings, 11.

40 Malcolm X, *The Autobiography of Malcolm X* (New York: Ballantine Books, 1964), 277–78.

41 Baker-Fletcher, 76–77.

42 Malcolm X, 253.

43 Baker-Fletcher, 76.

44 Jacquelyn Grant, "A Theological Framework," in *Working with Black Youth: Opportunities for Christian Ministry*, eds. Charles R. Foster and Grant S. Schockley (Nashville: Abingdon Press, 1989), 58–59.

45 J. Deotis Roberts, *The Prophethood of Black Believers: An African American Political Theology for Ministry* (Louisville: Westminster/John Knox Press, 1994), 77.

46 Delores Williams, *Sisters in the Wilderness: The Challenge of Womanist God-Talk* (Maryknoll, N.Y.: Orbis Books, 1993), 218–19.

47 Baker-Fletcher, 29.

48 Peter Paris, *The Social Teaching of the Black Churches* (Philadelphia: Fortress Press, 1985), 110.

49 Paris, *Social Teaching*, 111.

50 J. Deotis Roberts, *The Prophethood of Black Believers: An African American Political Theology for Ministry* (Louisville: Westminster/John Knox Press, 1994), 14.

51 Paris, *Social Teaching*, 112.

**Chapter 4**

52 Malcolm X, *The Autobiography of Malcolm X* (New York: Ballantine Books, 1964), 277–78.

53 C. Eric Lincoln and Lawrence H. Mamiya, *The Black Church in the African American Experience* (Durham: Duke University Press, 1990), 166–67.

54 Garth Baker-Fletcher, *Xodus: An African American Male Journey* (Minneapolis: Fortress Press, 1996), 76.

55 Tony Brown, *Black Lies, White Lies: The Truth According to Tony Brown* (New York: William Morrow and Co., 1995), 121.

56 Brown, 122.

57 Brown, 123.

58 Janice Hale-Benson, "Psychosocial Experiences," in *Working with Black Youth*, eds. Charles R. Foster and Grant S. Shockley (Nashville: Abingdon Press, 1989), 33–34.

59 Louise L. Hornor, ed., *Black Americans: A Statistical Sourcebook* (Palo Alto, Calif.: Information Publications, 1994), 23.

60 Wyatt Tee Walker, *The African-American Church and Economic Development* (New York: Martin Luther King Fellows Press, 1994), ix.

61 Wyatt Tee Walker, *African-American Church and Economic Development*, 26.

62 Wyatt Tee Walker, *African-American Church and Economic Development*, 28.

63 Wyatt Tee Walker, *African-American Church and Economic Development*, 22.

64 Wyatt Tee Walker, *African-American Church and Economic Development*, 44.

65 Wyatt Tee Walker, *African-American Church and Economic Development*, 30.

**Chapter 5**

66 Basil Moore, "What is Black Theology?" in *The Challenge of Black Theology in South Africa* (Atlanta: John Knox Press, 1973), 1.

67 Delores Williams, *Sisters in the Wilderness: The Challenge of Womanist God-Talk* (Maryknoll, N.Y.: Orbis Books, 1993), xiii.

68 Michael Eric Dyson, *Reflecting Black: African-American Cultural Criticism* (Minneapolis: University of Minnesota Press, 1993), 188.

69 Dyson, 187.

70 Theodore Walker, Jr., *Empower the People* (Maryknoll, N.Y.: Orbis Books, 1991), 65.

71 Theodore Walker, 65.

72 Josh Getlin, "Despite Pressure, NYPD Resists Call for Reforms," (Los Angeles: *The Los Angeles Times*, March 20, 2000).

73 Two books written by Edward Wimberly that are particularly helpful for African-American pastoral care are *African American Pastoral Care* (Nashville: Abingdon Press, 1991), and *Pastoral Counseling and Spiritual Values: A Black Point of View* (Nashville: Abingdon Press, 1982).

74 Richard H. Cobble, "Examining and Exploring Community and Church Initiatives that Provide Wholistic Approaches for Confronting Substance Abuse" (Ph.D. diss., Interdenominational Theological Center, 1995).

75 Deborah Prothrow-Stith and Michaele Weissman, *Deadly Consequences* (New York: HarperPerennial, 1991), 195.

76 Prothrow-Stith and Weissman, 195–96.

77 Prothrow-Stith and Weissman, 196.

78 C. Eric Lincoln and Lawrence H. Mamiya, *The Black Church in the African American Experience* (Durham: Duke University Press, 1990), 167.

**Chapter 6**

79 William J. Wilson, *The Truly Disadvantaged: The Inner City, The Underclass, and Public Policy* (Chicago: University of Chicago Press, 1987), 3–5.

80 U.S. Department of Commerce, Economics and Statistics Administration, *The National Data Book, Statistical Abstract of the United States 1998, 118th ed.* (Lakewood, Colorado: Bureau of the Census, 1998), 20–25.

**Chapter 7**

81 Ronald B. Mincy, editor, *Nurturing Young Black Males,* (Washington, D.C.: The Urban Institute Press, 1994), 104.

82 Clifford Geertz, *The Interpretation of Cultures,* (BasicBooks, A Division of HarperCollins Publishers, 1973), 45–46.

83 Social symbols influence and determine human behavior. A loss of social symbols will have an adverse impact upon human behavior. Clifford Geertz, *The Interpretation of Cultures* (Basic Books, 1973), 208.

84 Allen J. Beck, *Prisoners in 1999,* in Bureau Of Justice Statistics: Bulletin, U S. Department of Justice, Office of Justice Programs (Washington, DC: U.S. Department Of Justice, 2000), 10.

85 Peter J. Paris, "Moral Development for African-American Leadership," in *The Stones that the Builders Rejected, The Development of Ethical Leadership from the Black Church Tradition*, editor, Walter Earl Fluker (Harrisburg, Pennsylvania: Trinity Press International, 1998), 23–32.

86 Tony Brown, *Black Lies, White Lies, The Truth According to Tony Brown,* (New York: William Morrow and Company, Inc., 1995), 266–267.

87 Carter G. Woodson, *The Mis-Education of the Negro,* (New York: AMS Press, Inc. 1977), ix–xiv.

88 E. Franklin Frazier, *Black Bourgeoisie, The Rise of A New Middle Class,*(New York: The Free Press, Collier-Macmillan Limited, London, 1957), 10–13, 188–232.

89 Frazier, 9–26.

90 Carter G. Woodson, *The Mis-Education of the Negro,* (New York: AMS Press, Inc. 1977), 17–25.

91 Tony Brown, *Black Lies, White Lies, The Truth According to Tony Brown,* (New York: William Morrow and Company, Inc., 1995), 271.

92 Brown, 271.

93 Rev. Jesse L. Jackson, Sr., and Jesse L. Jackson, Jr., *It's About the Money!,* (New York: Times Books, 1999), 248.

94 Jackson and Jackson, 254–257.

95 Jimmy Swaggart Ministries, *Holy Bible, King James Version*, (Dallas, Texas: Heritage Publishers, Inc.), Luke Chapter 10: verse 27, p. 34 in New Testament.

# Bibliography

## *Books*


Abernathy, Ralph. *And the Walls Came Tumbling Down: Ralph David Abernathy—An Autobiography.* New York: Harper & Row, 1989.

Allen, Robert L. *Black Awakening in Capitalist America.* Trenton, N.J.: Africa World Press, 1990.

Ansbro, John J. *Martin Luther King, Jr.: The Making of a Mind.* Maryknoll, N.Y.: Orbis Books, 1982.

Ayres, Alex, ed. *The Wisdom of Martin Luther King.* New York: Penguin Group, 1993.

Baer, Hans A. *The Black Spiritual Movement: A Religious Response to Racism.* Knoxville: University of Tennessee Press, 1984.

Baker-Fletcher, Garth Kasimu. *Xodus: An African American Male Journey.* Minneapolis: Fortress Press, 1996.

Brown, Tony. *Black Lies, White Lies: The Truth According to Tony Brown.* New York: William Morrow and Co., 1995.

Cannon, Katie G. *Black Womanist Ethics.* Atlanta: Scholars Press, 1988.

Chapman, Mark L. *Christianity on Trial: African-American Religious Thought Before and After Black Power.* Maryknoll, N.Y.: Orbis Books, 1995.

Cone, James H. *Black Theology and Black Power.* San Francisco: Harper & Row, 1969.

———. *A Black Theology of Liberation.* 2nd ed. Maryknoll, N.Y.: Orbis Books, 1986.

———. *God of the Oppressed.* New York: Seabury Press, 1975.

———. *Martin and Malcolm and America: A Dream or a Nightmare.* Maryknoll, N.Y.: Orbis Books, 1991.

Cottman, Michael H. *Million Man March.* New York: Crown Trade Paperbacks, 1995.

Cummings, George C. L. *A Common Journey: Black Theology (USA) and Latin American Liberation Theology.* Maryknoll, N.Y.: Orbis Books, 1993.

Dyson, Michael Eric. *Reflecting Black: African-American Cultural Criticism.* Minneapolis: University of Minnesota Press, 1993.

Erskine, Noel Leo. *King among the Theologians.* Cleveland: Pilgrim Press, 1994.

Felder, Cain Hope. *Troubling Biblical Waters: Race, Class, Family.* Maryknoll, N.Y.: Orbis Books, 1989.

Foster, Charles R., ed. *Ethnicity in the Education of the Church.* Nashville: Scarritt Press, 1987.

Foster, Charles R., and Grant S. Shockley, eds. *Working with Black Youth: Opportunities for Christian Ministry.* Nashville: Abingdon Press, 1989.

Franklin, Robert Michael. *Liberating Visions: Human Fulfillment and Social Justice in African-American Thought.* Minneapolis: Fortress Press, 1990.

Freedman, Samuel G. *Upon this Rock: The Miracles of a Black Church.* New York: HarperPerennial, 1993.

Harrington, Michael. *The Other America: Poverty in the United States.* Middlesex, England: Penguin Books, 1981.

hooks, bell. *Black Looks: Race and Representation.* Boston: South End Press, 1992.

hooks, bell, and Cornel West. *Breaking Bread: Insurgent Black Intellectual Life.* Boston: South End Press, 1991.

Hornor, Louise L., ed. *Black Americans: A Statistical Sourcebook.* Palo Alto, Calif.: Information Publications, 1994.

Jackson, Jesse L., Sr. and Jesse L. Jackson, Jr. *It's About the Money!* New York: Times Books, 1999.

King, Coretta Scott. *The Words of Martin Luther King, Jr.* New York: Newmarket Press, 1983.

King, Martin Luther, Jr. *The Measure of a Man.* Philadelphia: Fortress Press, 1959.

———. *Strength to Love.* Philadelphia: Fortress Press, 1963.

———. *Stride Toward Freedom: The Montgomery Story.* New York: Harper & Row, 1958.

———. *Where Do We Go from Here: Chaos or Community?* Boston: Beacon Press, 1968.

———. *Why We Can't Wait.* New York: New American Library, 1964.

Lincoln, C. Eric. *Race, Religion, and the Continuing American Dilemma.* New York: Hill & Wang, 1984.

Lincoln, C. Eric, ed. *The Black Experience in Religion.* New York: Doubleday, 1974.

———. *Martin Luther King, Jr.: A Profile.* New York: Hill & Wang, 1970.

Lincoln, C. Eric, and Lawrence H. Mamiya. *The Black Church in the African American Experience* Durham: Duke University Press, 1990.

Mandela, Nelson. *Long Walk to Freedom: The Autobiography of Nelson Mandela.* Boston: Little, Brown and Company, 1995.

McCall, Nathan. *Makes Me Wanna Holler: A Young Black Man in America.* New York: Random House, 1994.

Moore, Basil, comp. *The Challenge of Black Theology in South Africa.* Atlanta: John Knox Press, 1973.

Paris, Peter. *Black Religious Leaders: Conflict in Unity.* 2nd ed. Louisville: Westminster/John Knox Press, 1991.

———. *The Social Teaching of the Black Churches.* Philadelphia: Fortress Press, 1985.

Ploski, Harry A., and James Williams, eds. *The Negro Almanac: A Reference Work on the African American.* 5th ed. New York: Gale Research, 1989.

Prothrow-Stith, Deborah, and Michaele Weissman. *Deadly Consequences.* New York: HarperPerennial, 1991.

Raboteau, Albert J. *Slave Religion: The "Invisible Institution" in the Antebellum South.* New York: Oxford University Press, 1978.

Roberts, J. Deotis. *The Prophethood of Black Believers: An African American Political Theology for Ministry.* Louisville: Westminster/John Knox Press, 1994.

Walker, Theodore, Jr. *Empower the People: Social Ethics for the African-American Church.* Maryknoll, N.Y.: Orbis Books, 1991.

Walker, Wyatt Tee. *The African-American Church and Economic Development.* New York: Martin Luther King Fellows Press, 1994.

———. *Afrocentrism and Christian Faith.* New York: Martin Luther King Fellows Press, 1993.

———. *The Soul of Black Worship.* New York: Martin Luther King Fellows Press, 1984.

West, Cornel. *Race Matters.* Boston: Beacon Press, 1993.

Williams, Delores S. *Sisters in the Wilderness: The Challenge of Womanist God-Talk.* Maryknoll, N.Y.: Orbis Books, 1993.

Wilmore, Gayraud S. *Black and Presbyterian: The Heritage and the Hope.* Philadelphia: Geneva Press, 1983.

———. *Black Religion and Black Radicalism.* 2nd ed. Maryknoll, N.Y.: Orbis Books, 1983.

Wilson, William J. *The Declining Significance of Race: Blacks and Changing American Institutions.* 2nd ed. Chicago: University of Chicago Press, 1980.

———. *The Truly Disadvantaged: The Inner City, the Underclass, and Public Policy.* Chicago: University of Chicago Press, 1987.

Wimberly, Edward P. *African American Pastoral Care.* Nashville: Abingdon Press, 1991.

———. *Pastoral Counseling and Spiritual Values: A Black Point of View.* Nashville: Abingdon Press, 1982.

X, Malcolm. *The Autobiography of Malcolm X.* New York: Ballantine Books, 1964.

## *Articles*

Biko, Steve. "Black Consciousness and the Quest for a True Humanity." In *The Challenge of Black Theology in South Africa.* Comp. Basil Moore. Atlanta: John Knox Press, 1973.

Grant, Jacquelyn. "A Theological Framework." In *Working with Black Youth: Opportunities for Christian Ministry.* Eds. Charles R. Foster and Grant S. Schockley. Nashville: Abingdon Press, 1989.

Hale-Benson, Janice. "Psychosocial Experiences." In *Working with Black Youth: Opportunities for Christian Ministry.* Eds. Charles R. Foster and Grant S. Shockley. Nashville: Abingdon Press, 1989.

Moore, Basil. "What is Black Theology?" In *The Challenge of Black Theology in South Africa.* Comp. Basil Moore. Atlanta: John Knox Press, 1973.

Moseley, Romney M. "Retrieving Intergenerational and Intercultural Faith." In *Working with Black Youth: Opportunities for Christian Ministry.* Eds. Charles R. Foster and Grant S. Shockley. Nashville: Abingdon Press, 1989.

### *Other Sources*

Cobble, Richard H. "Examining and Exploring Community and Church Initiatives that Provide Wholistic Approaches for Confronting Substance Abuse." Ph.D. diss., Interdenominational Theological Center, 1995.

Ivory, Luther. "Martin Luther King, Jr. as a Theologian of Radical Involvement." Ph.D. diss., Emory University, 1996.

# Index

K



L



M



N



O



P

# Research in Religion and Family
## BLACK PERSPECTIVES

This series aims to provide a framework and opportunity for original research that explores both the ground and the goals of family and religion in the black tradition. Monographs in the series will examine the ways in which kinship networks were formed and maintained, how the community raised and socialized children, how they carved out a religion and fashioned a rich and expressive culture that reflected their uninhibited imagination and provided a means to articulate their hopes and hurts, their dreams and doubts.

Research will not only focus on the past and present, but will also look at the adequacy of current models of family and religion to take the black community into the twenty-first century.

The series editor is:

Noel Leo Erskine
Candler School of Theology
Emory University
Atlanta, GA 30322

To order other books in this series, please contact our Customer Service Department:

(800) 770-LANG (within the U.S.)
(212) 647-7706 (outside the U.S.)
(212) 647-7707 FAX

Or browse online by series:

www.peterlangusa.com